To Steve,
All the best,
Bruce Paulsen

Out of the Fog

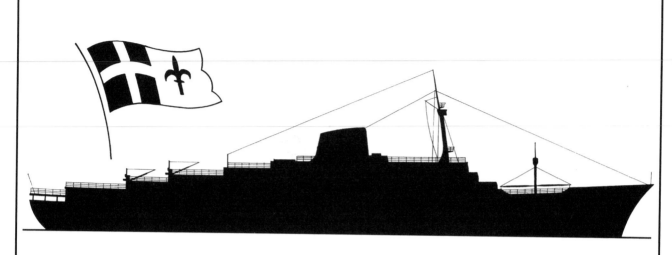

Andrea Doria
Societa Navigatione, Genoa

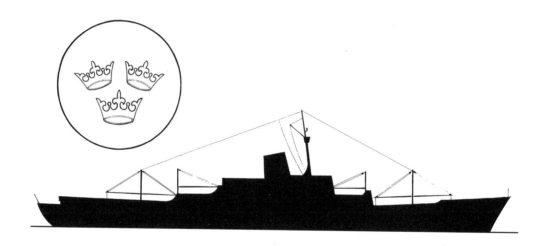

Stockholm
Swedish America Line, Gothenburg

Out of the Fog
The Sinking of *Andrea Doria*

Algot Mattsson

**English translation edited
by Gordon W. Paulsen
and Bruce G. Paulsen**

*Translated from the Swedish
by Richard E. Fisher*

CORNELL MARITIME PRESS
Centreville, Maryland

Originally published in Sweden by Tre Böcker as *Den Långa Natten:* Andrea Doria*'s Undergång* (*The Long Night: The Sinking of* Andrea Doria), by Algot Mattsson, with the assistance of Third Mate Johan-Ernst Carstens-Johannsen

Library of Congress Cataloging-in-Publication Data

Mattsson, Algot.
 [Den långa natten. English]
 Out of the fog : the sinking of Andrea Doria / Algot Mattsson ;
English translation edited by Gordon W. Paulsen and Bruce G. Paulsen ;
translated from the Swedish by Richard E. Fisher.
      p. cm.
Includes bibliographical references (p.) and an index.
 ISBN 0-87033-545-6 (hardcover)
 1. Andrea Doria (Steamship) 2. Stockholm (Motorship) 3.
Shipwrecks—North Atlantic Ocean. I. Paulsen, Gordon W. II. Paulsen,
Bruce G., 1958- III. Title.
 G530.A244M3813 2003
 363.12'3'0916346—dc21
                                2002155927

Manufactured in the United States of America
First American edition

To my wife Janet and in honor of my two chief mentors in the field of maritime law, Professor Nicholas J. Healy and the late Charles S. Haight.

—G.W.P.

To my wife Barbara and to my parents.

—B.G.P.

Contents

PREFACE

American Edition

It has been over forty-five years since the *Stockholm–Andrea Doria* collision occurred. At the time, the event was regarded as an ominous augury signaling a less-than-glowing future for transoceanic passenger service. While it may have marked the beginning of the end of regular liner service across the oceans, it certainly was not the end of passenger ships. Ocean cruises are the vacation of choice for large numbers of people who annually schedule cruises on luxury passenger ships that have every amenity. See the Sunday travel section of any major American paper for examples of the endless variety of ocean cruises which are now offered to the public. New passenger vessels are put into service every year to satisfy the traveling public's thirst for ocean vacations.

I first learned about the *Stockholm–Andrea Doria* collision on the morning of July 26, 1956, when I drove my late law partner, Richard G. Ashworth, to the railroad station. He had spent the night with us at our home in Douglaston, New York. In those days of non-air-conditioned commuter trains, Dick had to yell through an open railroad car window to tell me about the

collision and to urge me to buy a newspaper. I did, and my life changed dramatically from that moment on. I called my mentor Charles S. Haight, a senior partner at the law firm where I was employed at the time, and he told me that the firm, Haight Gardner Poor and Havens, had been retained to represent the owner and underwriters of *Stockholm* in this case. I interrupted my vacation and set to work to do anything required of me. What ensued for me were the most exciting and action-filled days and nights that any young maritime lawyer could experience. Working so closely with my partners and associates was truly a learning experience of the first magnitude and of incalculable value to me. I know the firm's clients in this case were well served, and the manner in which the case was concluded was a prime example of how litigants in a high-profile maritime case can settle the issue without resorting to mutual character assassination.

I did not know of the publication of Algot Mattsson's book about the collision until I visited Sweden some five years ago. I was made aware of it through Erik Hedborg of the Swedish Protection and Indemnity

Association, with whom Charles Haight and I had worked on the *Andrea Doria–Stockholm* collision case. I met Carstens, who kindly gave me an inscribed copy of the book. I read it through hastily. My father was Swedish and my mother Norwegian, so I have some knowledge of the Nordic languages, although not enough to make an accurate translation in any one of them.

I concluded that because the book contained information that had been available only to those with reading knowledge of Swedish, the book ought to be translated into English. Hedborg agreed. I asked my friend, Professor Richard Fisher of Lund University in Sweden, to make a translation, which he expertly did.

A word of caution: as all trial lawyers know, it is practically impossible to reconcile testimony by many witnesses to every aspect of any one incident. The *Stockholm–Andrea Doria* collision is no exception to this rule, so it is inevitable that there will be some inconsistencies in the text.

My deepest thanks to all who have been helpful in this project, particularly my secretary, Caroline Fitzgerald McLoughlin, and Dorothy Donnelly, a paralegal in my firm, who have both done excellent work for me. My son Bruce's secretary, Susan Ciardullo, was also very helpful in preparing the text. I am especially grateful to my senior partner, Nicholas J. Healy, who kindly read and critiqued the book.

I want to thank my beloved wife, Janet, for bearing with me through the arduous preparation of this book, and I wish to thank her and our children—my coeditor Bruce, and Faith and Emily—for proofreading the text.

I apologize for any errors which may inadvertently appear.

—Gordon W. Paulsen

First (Swedish) Edition

It was 2300 eastern daylight saving time on July 25, 1956. Unbeknown to the crews aboard either vessel, two of the world's most modern passenger ships were speeding toward each other in the vicinity of *Nantucket* lightship off the East Coast of the United States. One vessel was *Andrea Doria,* the pride of the Italian fleet. The other was *Stockholm,* the Swedish fleet's newest vessel, though by no means its finest.

Ten minutes later one of the worst maritime catastrophes in history occurred, measured not by the number of lives lost, but in monetary value. Eleven hours after the collision, *Andrea Doria* sank along North America's coastline after a night of tense drama.

After dipping her flag to the sinking *Andrea Doria,* the heavily damaged *Stockholm,* which had lost a large portion of her bow, returned to New York Harbor carrying a large number of survivors from *Andrea Doria.*

The long night's horror was over at a cost of fifty-one dead from the Italian passenger ship and five from *Stockholm.* In addition, numerous injuries were suffered by persons who were rescued, and material damage was heavy.

The famous *Lutine* bell in the Lloyd's of London insurance office sounded the death knell of *Andrea Doria* the next morning in accordance with a long-standing tradition. It was just the beginning of the mass media coverage of an occurrence that was in the same category of newsworthy events of the year 1956 as the Suez Canal crisis and the USSR's crushing of the freedom movement in Hungary. Even thirty years after the event, the *Stockholm–Andrea Doria* collision was regarded as one of the ten most dramatic events of the postwar era.

Many important questions remain unanswered even now. How could a collision occur between two vessels on the open sea, when they had practically unlimited turning room and were both equipped with the most modern technical gear? Who was to blame for the collision? How could the "unsinkable" *Andrea Doria* go down?

A preliminary hearing—which had been held in New York and which would have led to a court trial if a settlement had not been worked out—began on September 19, 1956, and was terminated on January 24, 1957. No definitive answer to these questions had yet been given. Some of the witnesses had not been heard, and a number of important documents had not been presented.

The Swedish America Line, owner of *Stockholm,* and the Italian Line, owner of *Andrea Doria,* settled without court proceedings in order to avoid all the publicity that claims and counterclaims would elicit and that—no matter who was found to be at fault—would result in reduced public confidence in the two shipowners and in passenger ships in general.

The result of an actual court proceeding can only be speculated. However, it is clear that both parties had trump cards that were held in reserve for possible use in a trial. Some of these cards are revealed for the first time in this book. The persons who were aboard *Andrea Doria* and *Stockholm* that long night of July 25 and 26, 1956, would never forget the disaster.

For the highly qualified skipper of *Andrea Doria,* Piero Calamai, the catastrophe also became a personal tragedy. He felt the loss of his ship deeply, and he was in poor physical condition when he arrived in New York. During the hearing, he did not wear his uniform; he no longer had the confidence of his employer, the Italian Line. He never again went to sea, even though it had been planned that he would be master of Italian Line's newest ship, *Cristoforo Colombo.* The voyage to New York was to have been his last aboard *Andrea Doria* before taking over the newer sister ship.

Captain Calamai's daughters stated that their father, when he got back to Genoa after the hearings were finished in New York, strolled on the pier with his head down and seemed to be in mourning "like a father who has lost his sons."

For those who had been in charge of *Stockholm,* the situation was quite different. Captain Gunnar Nordenson was promoted to be master of Swedish America Line's newest ship, *Gripsholm,* which was being built in the Ansaldo Shipyard in Genoa, the same yard that built *Andrea Doria.* Third Mate Johan-Ernst Carstens-Johannsen, who had been on watch on *Stockholm* at the time of the collision, followed Captain Nordenson and became third mate on *Gripsholm.*

During many conversations with Captain Nordenson (who lived in Gothenburg and died in 1981 at the age of eighty-eight), it was clear that he never, for a second, doubted that he and this third mate Carstens had handled matters correctly when *Stockholm* and *Andrea Doria* met off Nantucket.

Neither of the vessels was officially exonerated inasmuch as the court hearing came to no conclusion. However, the settlement between Swedish America Line and Italian Line sent a clear message. The Italian Line had to bear its own losses—the loss of *Andrea Doria,* valued at $30 million— while Swedish America Line had to pay for the repair of *Stockholm,* which came to about $1 million. The insurers became the "great professor" because the allocation of damages in its own way indicated the answer to the questions concerning the degree of fault of each ship. Though Italian Line had not stood by its best known and most knowledgeable shipmaster, Swedish America Line's trust in Captain Nordenson and third mate Carstens-Johannsen could not be misinterpreted.

The testimony of then third mate Carstens-Johannsen during the hearing in New York is part of nautical history. However, Carstens (as he was known by his friends) had in the ensuing years refused to express himself about anything other than what was said at the hearing.

In this book, Carstens for the first time states his opinion and gives details not only about how the collision came about, but also about how he reacted as the one solely responsible on the bridge of *Stockholm.* What happened during the next hours, days, and months? How did life change for this happy, extroverted, but at the same time, conscientious twenty-six-year-old who happened to play the principal role in this maritime drama?

Carstens, just like Captain Nordenson, never doubted that he had acted properly. Carstens had obeyed all the rules that apply to vessels at sea. The responsible persons on *Andrea Doria* had not done so.

Carstens commented sharply, "It was, after all, *Andrea Doria* which as the result of her strange maneuvers sailed into *Stockholm,* not the other way round, as is so often stated."

Captain Calamai was one of the key persons on the Italian side when it became necessary to explain why he undertook the maneuvers which led to the collision. The record of the court proceeding was studied carefully, by the Italian Line and at the offices of the Swedish America Line in Gothenburg. There were many questions but few answers.

After the initial hearing, Captain Calamai never again expressed himself about the collision. He had been ordered by Italian Line to keep quiet. Reporters' questions were left unanswered, and his family said that he not once, not even for his wife and children, related what had happened or how the collision could have been avoided.

Captain Calamai had been master of *Andrea Doria* since her maiden voyage, and he naturally knew she had a stability problem. At the hearing in New York, he said that the most important ship's documents of all had not been saved. How this could have happened was never explained and is a secret he took with him to his grave.

Other failures on the part of *Andrea Doria* were kept quiet and not included in the testimony. The Italian Line had nothing to gain by discussions concerning *Andrea Doria*'s stability or errors in the ship's construction. Such would only hurt the passenger business of the Italian Line and, most importantly, *Andrea Doria*'s sister ship, *Cristoforo Colombo.*

But despite the silence of Italian Line, there were flaws in construction, and they are revealed here for the first time. These flaws became fatal when *Stockholm* and *Andrea Doria* met just off the East Coast of North America.

—Algot Mattsson
Gothenburg, Sweden, 1986

Out of the Fog

CHAPTER 1

Two Very Different Ships

Two quite dissimilar ships met forcibly off Nantucket on the night of July 25 and 26, 1956. *Andrea Doria* was one of the most luxurious and most prestigious vessels to emerge during the period following World War II. The prewar Italian fleet was but a memory. Its great ships had mostly been pulverized by the planes and submarines of the Allied forces as the Italian vessels tried desperately to maintain connections between the homeland and its warring troops in North Africa.

The luxury liners *Rex* and *Conte di Savoia*—created during the reign of Mussolini and extravagantly adorned with works of art and fine furnishings—were the pride of Italy prior to the war. When they were gone, postwar Italy tried to reconstitute what had been lost. The goal was for the sister ships *Andrea Doria* and *Cristoforo Colombo* to recapture a place for that great seafaring nation on the oceans of the world. *Andrea Doria* was the first big postwar Italian passenger ship on the North Atlantic run. Boarding her was an entrance to the gorgeous world of the Renaissance. When she docked in New York on her maiden voyage, one ship designer wrote the following: "Her name is *Andrea Doria*. She is the most beautiful example of modern naval architecture I have ever seen."

Andrea Doria represented not only the new art of shipbuilding in the postwar period, but also the persistent belief that people would continue to prefer to travel between Europe and America aboard ships.

Stockholm was the antithesis of *Andrea Doria*. She was created as a hybrid totally unlike Swedish America Line's prewar *Kungsholm* and *Gripsholm*—something between a passenger liner and a freighter but in practice, neither one nor the other.

According to her owner, Swedish America Line, *Stockholm* was intended to be a "transitional" ship, a response to the languishing transatlantic traffic. Her purpose was to underscore the transition of means of transport, allowing the airlines to gradually assume the increasing stream of passenger traffic across the North Atlantic.

Yet, for *Andrea Doria*, which was placed in transatlantic service in 1953 (five years later than *Stockholm*), the assumptions were quite different. For the Italian people, she was more significant than any of her predecessors. After all, over half of the country's

Data	*Andrea Doria* (top)	*Stockholm* (bottom)
Builder	Ansaldo Yard, Genoa	Göta Yard, Gothenburg
Tonnage	29,083	12,165
Length	700 feet	525 feet
Speed	23 knots	18 knots
Passenger capacity	1,221	570 (after rebuilding)
Maiden voyage	January 14, 1953	February 21, 1948

ships had been destroyed during the Second World War, and *Andrea Doria* represented the rebirth of Italy as a leading seafaring nation.

By 1955, the restructuring of Italian shipping was largely complete. Italian Line carried more than a hundred thousand passengers between America and Europe, surpassed only by Cunard White Star Line of Britain. This same high capacity was carried the following year. Since *Andrea Doria* was Italy's "firstborn" on the North Atlantic after the war, she was embraced with the same devotion as the eldest son in an Italian family.

For all these reasons, the announcement of her sinking came as a shock to the Italian people. The size of the ship was never questioned in Italy. Her mission was to carry on the proud traditions of the prewar period. When she was launched on June 16, 1951, at the Ansaldo Shipyard in Genoa—a shipyard boasting nearly a hundred years of shipbuilding tradition—and christened *Andrea Doria,* there was no end to the public jubilation. For on such a day, who could resist reliving the glory of one of Genoa's greatest heroes of the sea, the man who had liberated the city from French domination in 1528? For that achievement, Admiral Andrea Doria had been given the honorary titles of "Censor (Judge) for Life" and "Father and Liberator of the Fatherland." In their time, the Dorias and three related families were called "the four great families of Genoa." Even today, three large palaces in the city testify to the Doria family's power and prestige.

Hence, it was perfectly natural that one of the largest of the new, postwar passenger ships should be named for Genoa's great hero of naval warfare and that her somewhat younger sister ship should receive her name from another of the famous sons of Genoa—Christopher Columbus.

The 1950s were a golden decade for passenger companies on the North Atlantic. In addition to *Andrea Doria, Cristoforo Colombo,* and *Stockholm,* other newcomers at this time included *Kungsholm,* built at Vlissingen in the Netherlands; the second *Gripsholm,* built in Genoa; and the American vessels *Independence, Constitution,* and *United States.* The passenger fleet was further expanded during the late 1950s by an additional sixteen ships in a range of sizes and with diverse amenities.

Swedish America Line had the advantage of greeting the end of hostilities with at least part of its passenger fleet intact. The first *Stockholm* had been built at the Monfalcone Shipyard in Italy at the end of the 1930s, but she was never taken over by the Swedes; she had been sold to the Italian government at a good profit. *Kungsholm,* delivered to Swedish America Line in 1928, had been sold to the United States. She served as a troop transport under the name *John Ericsson.* What remained—still in relatively good condition—were *Drottningholm,* purchased in 1920, and the original *Gripsholm,* built in 1925. New ships were needed. The money was there from previous sales, so no economic reason would prevent building a vessel more in accordance with Swedish America Line's prewar traditions.

The company's organization in America expected an explosive increase in the demand for travel over the Atlantic once the war finally ended. This potential growth presented the opportunity to revive the cruise traffic in which Swedish America Line had formerly enjoyed world leadership. At the main office of Swedish America Line in Gothenburg, there was absolute certainty that the demand for travel between Europe and America would grow like wildfire. On both sides of the Atlantic, people had a dammed-up desire to visit relatives, and as the German troops were taking over the heart of Europe, millions of people were being displaced. As so often occurred in the past during times of war and misfortune, America was considered "the promised land."

Yet, for the directors of Swedish America Line, these positive indicators were of no significance. The new *Stockholm*, ordered from Götaverken in Gothenburg on October 11, 1944—seven months before the end of the war in Europe—became Swedish America Line's "bastard." Throughout the entire time of her building, there were internal disagreements among the directors and the executive management in both Gothenburg and New York. With no traditions from the past, the ship was considered by some to be an unwelcome newcomer in the White Viking Fleet, as the company's ships were known.

The decision to build *Stockholm*, once finally reached, was accompanied by no fanfare. Everyone familiar with passenger traffic knew that the directors had made a historic mistake, one that would, in the coming years, cost the company at least 30 million Swedish krona. Just possibly, the new ship signaled the beginning of the end for a shipping company that, in the final phases of the war, had seemed to hold all the advantages.

When completed, *Stockholm* could carry more than the 200 passengers indicated on her original plan, but she still had the smallest tonnage on the North Atlantic. It is often suggested that a ship's misfortune begins on the slipway. Surely many people recalled this old truism when the great catastrophe occurred off Nantucket, since *Stockholm* was dogged by bad luck right from the outset. First, the laying of the keel had been delayed for several months because of a strike of the Metal Workers' Union. Later, when the christening was finally scheduled for September 9, 1946, she stubbornly refused to obey Ann-Ida Broström's directive to enter her proper element. Many tense minutes passed for all the parties involved before *Stockholm* ever so slowly inched down

the ways. That delay was thought to be a bad omen.

Andrea Doria and *Stockholm* had one thing in common: both were unstable. Not, of course, when checked by international laws and regulations with respect to safety at sea. *Stockholm* measured up to these with a good margin to spare. *Andrea Doria* also met the requirements, but only under specific circumstances.

However, special factors were noted on the Swedish ship, and these factors must constantly be taken into the picture. "She rolls like an eggshell" was a frequent observation from passengers who had experienced her unpredictable movements even in relatively smooth seas. In attempting to deal with this careening from side to side, the cargo holds, originally intended for express freight, were filled with three thousand tons of stone. The addition of this weight brought very limited success. As far as the construction of her bottom was concerned, *Stockholm* was not built to guarantee a calm voyage across a restless North Atlantic. It was only when stabilizers were installed a few months before the collision with *Andrea Doria* that a more comfortable sea voyage could be offered. That change was really overdue! After eight years, *Stockholm* had received a solid reputation as one of the very worst "rockers" on the Atlantic.

The design of *Andrea Doria,* both above and below the waterline, differed significantly from that of *Stockholm,* but her stability had been seriously questioned right from the modeling stage. Toward the end of her voyages across the Atlantic, when both the oil and freshwater tanks in her bottom had been emptied, she rolled precariously. Even during sudden swerves, *Andrea Doria* had a tendency to assume a list that the stability experts apparently had not foreseen. With regard to the possibility of staying afloat after a collision, both *Stockholm* and *Andrea Doria* had shown certain characteristics that differentiated them. *Stockholm*, the older of the two ships, would be able to stay afloat no matter which of her nine holds were filled with water. However, if one of the sections between the watertight bulkheads should spring a leak, it would be extremely hazardous to proceed.

In 1948 regulations were sharpened for all passenger ships whose keels were laid after that year. For *Andrea Doria* this meant, among other things, that she was designed so she should not sink, even if two of the eleven separate sections between her watertight bulkheads were to be filled. Because of this design, *Andrea Doria* was regarded as "unsinkable." But unfortunately that assumption was only a theory. In practice, the Italian luxury liner had built-in defects that nullified the watertight bulkheads and proved to be fatal flaws.

Both *Stockholm* and *Andrea Doria* had experienced difficulties on their maiden voyage. On February 21, 1948, after much delay, *Stockholm* was finally ready to make her first voyage across the North Atlantic. It was an uneasy trip, and the passengers could ascertain quite early on that crossing the Atlantic at that time of year would be no bed of roses. The infamous winter storms tested *Stockholm* severely. Even the passengers with the best sea legs quickly felt the results of *Stockholm*'s capriciousness. One passenger died during a severe storm, which naturally aroused trepidation on board and enforced the opinion that *Stockholm* was a very unstable ship.

Almost exactly five years later in January 1953, *Andrea Doria* was ready for delivery and set out on her maiden voyage. The usual route after leaving her home port of Genoa was to stop at the ports of Cannes, Naples, and Gibraltar before heading out past the Azores toward her final destination, New York.

As was the case for *Stockholm*, *Andrea Doria*'s maiden voyage was very troublesome.

Off the East Coast of the United States— precisely in the waters where the sea drama of July 25 and 26, 1956, was to transpire— *Andrea Doria* ran into a violent storm. She was hit broadside by a huge wave and recorded a list of 28°. Many people on board, both passengers and crew, were tossed about, and twenty people were injured. The reaction to this sudden and violent broadside intimated that *Andrea Doria*'s stability was not up to par, at least not when her fuel and ballast water tanks were nearly empty toward the end of a voyage.

Stockholm and *Andrea Doria* were opposites, both outside and inside, though they had one thing in common: both had only one smokestack, which would have been unthinkable some decades earlier when the number of stacks indicated the status of a ship. Southern European emigrants, in particular, were said to be extremely uneasy about traveling across the Atlantic on a ship that did not have several smokestacks emitting great clouds of smoke. They believed that safety at sea depended on the number of smokestacks—at least they were encouraged to believe so by competing companies.

However, after World War II, radical changes had been made in the design of ships. Streamlining became the highest fashion, from a sharply falling bow to a rounded superstructure and a spoon-shaped stern. A slender mast and a smokestack leaning aft further accentuated the sense of a rapid crossing by a ship over a great expanse of water.

The exteriors of the two ships showed many differences. The original *Stockholm*, before her superstructure was enlarged to contain additional cabins and a movie theater, looked more like a cruise ship than a passenger liner. And despite her modern external design, *Andrea Doria* still displayed certain features of a traditional passenger liner, particularly her massive superstructure, which actually created a palpable risk.

Even though her builders had employed mostly lightweight alloys, nothing could prevent the ship from being top-heavy. When not properly ballasted, she would lose stability.

When Swedish America Line built *Stockholm*, it was constantly emphasized that she was to be a ship characterized more by comfort than by luxury. When she was completed and displayed for the press, no one contradicted the company on that point. *Stockholm* was entirely lacking in the traditional luxury that had formerly made a voyage across the Atlantic something special—a dream, a memory for life. One expert in ship design wrote: "*Stockholm*'s public spaces do not differ very much from the appointments of a modern provincial café." This judgment was harsh, but not without reason, if one compared her with earlier ships whose entire atmosphere reminded the passengers they were indeed experiencing the best of everything.

However, it would be wrong to ignore certain qualities of *Stockholm*'s interior design, particularly one of history-making significance. Before the work on the interior appointments got underway, Swedish America Line built a number of "test cabins" in full scale. These test cabins were complemented with furniture, ventilation devices, and surrounding passageways. The company tested these cabins over and over again, redesigned them, and finally came up with an overall design for all decks that made it possible for every cabin to face outward. What this meant in practice was that everyone on board *Stockholm*, passengers and crew alike, was berthed in a "room with an ocean view."

Swedish America Line received much praise for this arrangement. Even though the "windows" might not be very large, their presence counteracted the depressing, claustrophobic feeling that many people had previously experienced from lacking contact with the outside world. As far as the crew was concerned, this was a "revolution on the Atlantic."

Andrea Doria was a ship of contrasts in terms of the appointments and locations of her cabins. In order to accommodate 1,221 passengers and 570 crewmembers, it was impossible to build outside cabins for all. The six decks housing the passenger cabins revealed great differences, ranging from the foyer deck's four luxury suites to the C deck's conglomeration of cabins in eight rows straight across the entire breadth of the ship. In an advertising brochure, Italian Line described *Andrea Doria* as the ship of graceful lines, expansive sunny decks, and an unusually beautiful interior. It went on: "First and foremost, a ship must function as an enormous machine that provides her passengers with light, heat, and hotel service. She must cleave the ocean waves smoothly and safely under all weather conditions. But she must be more than that: she must be an entire lifestyle for her passengers—an experience they will revel in while they have it and that they will never forget as long as they live. *Andrea Doria* is, in our opinion, unique. She was built as a living testimonial to the importance of beauty in our daily lives."

Indeed, *Andrea Doria* was unique in many ways. She was like a world unto herself in which thirty-one lounges were individually created to allow free scope for personal preferences. But it was her architectural and artistic embellishments that made *Andrea Doria* famous around the world.

When passengers and visitors went on board, they encountered the magnificence of the Renaissance: huge murals, frescoes, tapestries, sculptures, and mirrors. These were all originals, not copies. The finest work of art, regarded as invaluable, had been painted by Salvadore Fiume, and it filled the five hundred square meters of wall space in the first-class lounge. In the middle of the lounge stood a bronze statue

There were three classes on board *Andrea Doria*—first, cabin, and tourist. On *Stockholm*, there were two—first and tourist. The photo shows the drawing room aboard *Andrea Doria*.

of the legendary Admiral Andrea Doria, dressed in full armor. The Doria family's coat of arms hung above the statue, a gift to the ship from the Marquis Giambattista Doria. As viewed from the Swedish perspective, all these appointments and artistic adornments might have seemed a bit pompous, but by and large, they reflected a historical course of events that the Italians, in this postwar period, felt a need to reexperience, albeit in their dreams.

In their advertisements in America, the Italian company often emphasized the opportunities for tourists to travel to Europe in a ship that took the "sunshine route."

Passengers could experience summer already on the trip across the Atlantic by choosing "the southern route," but this choice would be an unlikely one for those traveling to a northern European harbor. Consequently, *Andrea Doria* was, for the most part, equipped for the outdoor life. When she was built, she was the only ship in the world that boasted three swimming pools on her decks, each nicely decorated with tables and sun umbrellas, equipped with bars and staffed by waiters in white jackets. Even poor emigrants could feel like millionaires for a few days on such premises. No wonder the Italians wept when this ship went down.

To enter the first-class drawing room aboard *Andrea Doria* was to experience the beauty of the Renaissance world. These photographs show the salon from two different angles.

In the center of the great salon stood a bronze statue of Admiral Andrea Doria, naval hero and Genoa's emancipator.

World famous Italian cuisine was enjoyed in *Andrea Doria*'s first-class dining room, while children enjoyed meals in their own dining area.

On board *Andrea Doria,* nothing was spared in decorating the first-class children's playroom. The same was true of the bedroom in a luxury suite.

The swimming pool on deck was very popular; a picture of *Andrea Doria*'s first-class pool is shown. The bottom photo shows the second-class dining salon.

Even the children's playroom in second class was richly decorated. All the works of art on board *Andrea Doria* were original.

While not every cabin on *Andrea Doria* had portholes, many—even in second class—were roomy and pleasant.
In the swimming pool area, there were bars on the open deck.

Andrea Doria's chapel with its beautiful altar was visited often.

OUT OF THE FOG

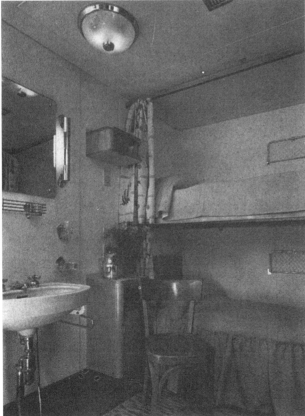

Andrea Doria's third-class dining salon was more sparsely furnished, but still quite comfortable when compared with similar prewar ships. Sections of C Deck and forward were not as comfortable, as shown in the photo of a third-class cabin.

Cross section

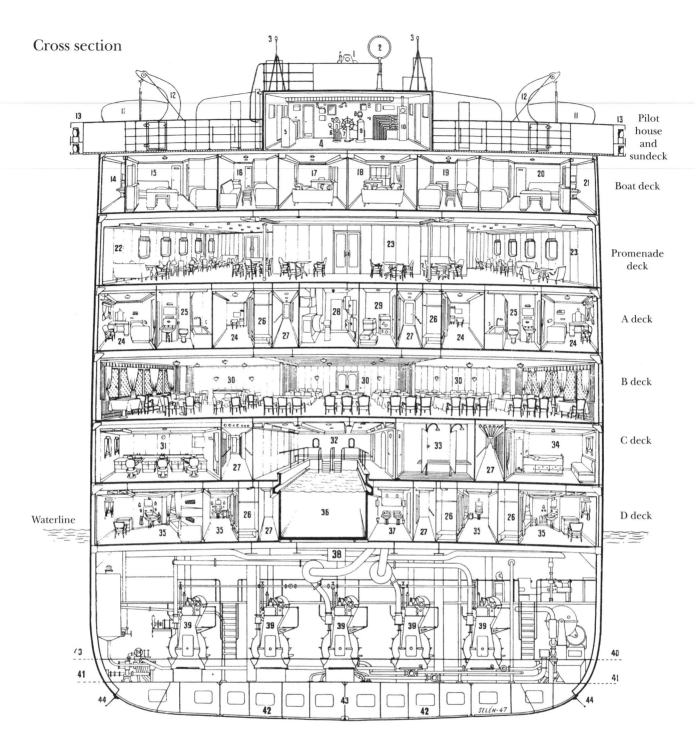

Pilot house and sundeck

Boat deck

Promenade deck

A deck

B deck

C deck

Waterline

D deck

1. Standard compass	12. Lifeboat davits	23. First-class drawing room	34. Single cabin for crewmember
2. Bearing scope	13. Sidelight	24. First-class cabins	35. Tourist-class cabin
3. Morse lamps	14. Chief officer's toilet	25. Bathroom for first-class cabins	36. Swimming pool
4. Wheelhouse	15. Chief officer's cabin	26. Closet	37. Women's toilet
5. Radar	16. Captain's sleeping cabin	27. Corridor	38 Auxiliary engine room
6. Steering compass	17. Captain's day cabin	28. AC room	39. Auxiliary engine
7. Telemotor	18. Chief engineer's day cabin	29. Baggage room	40. Engine room deck
8. Gyro compass	19. Chief engineer's sleeping cabin	30. Dining room	41. Double-bottom tank top
9. Automatic steering	20. First engineer's sleeping cabin	31. Beauty parlor	42. Bottom tanks
10. Smoke detector	21. First engineer's toilet room	32. Swimming pool	43. Cooling
11. Lifeboats	22. First-class bar	33. Shower room	44. Keel

The drawing room on *Stockholm* was not as luxurious as that on *Andrea Doria*. Still it was the most luxurious room in first class and occupied the entire breadth of the ship. The relatively small first-class dining room in the bottom photo suffers in comparison with the drawing room.

TWO VERY DIFFERENT SHIPS

Stockholm had only two classes. The top photo shows the second-class writing room and the bottom photo, a cabin in first class.

OUT OF THE FOG

The second-class veranda and bar were the most popular rooms on *Stockholm*, the smallest passenger ship plying the Atlantic.

CHAPTER 2

Skippers with Spotless Records

Two experienced captains met off Nantucket on the night of July 25 and 26, 1956. Both had come up through the ranks, and both were very familiar with duties at sea. Captain Gunnar Nordenson of *Stockholm* was born in Quincy, Massachusetts, in 1893 but returned to Sweden with his parents while still a child. He often spoke proudly about his American connections.

Gunnar Nordenson went to sea in 1911 at the age of eighteen and received his captain's certificate in 1918. He was employed by Swedish America Line in 1920 and subsequently served in various positions on nearly all of its passenger liners. For three years during World War II, he was in command of the first *Gripsholm,* which was engaged in the exchange of wounded soldiers and diplomats between the warring parties. He received several honors for his accomplishments.

Captain Nordenson was not in command when *Stockholm* made her maiden voyage in 1948. He first joined her for a three-month period in 1954 and returned on September 14, 1955. Among other duties, Captain Nordenson was assigned to command Swedish America Line's long cruises. He was known for having precisely the qualities required for the social life on board.

Like so many of his peers at the time, Captain Nordenson made an imprint on the atmosphere of the ships he commanded, not through a harsh regimen, but through conduct that conveyed respect toward all of his subordinates. He was always available for those who needed his support, if that support was justified. His untiring defense of Johan-Ernst Carstens-Johannsen during the preliminary hearing in New York was a fine example of this trait. Nordenson died in 1981 at the age of eighty-eight.

Captain Piero Calamai of *Andrea Doria* was described as "trustworthy and reserved." On occasion he could seem overly retiring as he consciously sought to avoid the official entertaining expected of the captain of a passenger liner. His place at the captain's table was often vacant.

Captain Calamai had commanded *Andrea Doria* from her maiden voyage in 1953, except for some time off for vacations. The fifty-eight-year-old captain was a skipper of the old school who did not always trust modern devices for navigational assistance. He relied more on the evidence

Gunnar Nordenson

Piero Calamai

Both ship captains had long and very distinguished careers, Gunnar Nordenson with Swedish America Line and Piero Calamai with the Italian Line. Neither of them had been involved in a serious casualty before the collision.

of his own eyes than on complicated instrumentation. He did not reject the new aids that were provided, but he left their operation to his subordinates, possibly because of his own lack of knowledge.

Captain Calamai graduated from the College of Navigation in Genoa as an eighteen-year-old. Navigation was part of his heritage—his father had founded a respected navigation journal. His brother was an admiral, and Captain Calamai himself had served in the navy during World War II. After the war, Captain Calamai had commanded various ships, and when he assumed his post on *Andrea Doria*, his career advanced rapidly.

This voyage with *Andrea Doria* was in any case intended to be the last one for Captain

Calamai. It had already been decided that he would assume command of another Italian Line vessel, *Cristoforo Colombo*.

The loss of *Andrea Doria* was a great personal tragedy for Captain Calamai. He was a broken man, even as the preliminary hearing got underway in New York. People who had first met him immediately after *Andrea Doria* went down and who saw him again a few months later maintained that he had aged several years in that brief interim.

The most deplorable outcome for Captain Calamai was that unlike Captain Nordenson, he was not entrusted to take over as the captain of a new ship. He was denounced by his employers, even though a proper trial was never held.

CHAPTER 3

Young, but Not Inexperienced

As the commanding officer of *Stockholm*, Captain Gunnar Nordenson had the ultimate responsibility on board. He had been standing on the bridge as *Stockholm* left New York, but when the ship approached Nantucket, Nordenson was in his cabin. Third Mate Johan-Ernst Carstens-Johannsen had taken over the watch.

Carstens was born on March 7, 1930. His father Ernst was the chief municipal medical officer in Lund; other members of his family were his mother Karin and his older siblings Minna and Hans. At the age of sixteen, Carstens left school and went to sea. He sampled the advantages and drawbacks of life at sea on board *Sunbeam*, a schooner once owned by the tea magnate Thomas Lipton. When Carstens sailed her, she was owned by the Rydberg Foundation and served as a training ship for future officers in the Swedish merchant fleet.

Carstens sandwiched studies at the Naval College in Gothenburg and the Navigation College in Malmö with practice on board the cargo ships of the Broström Group. In 1952 he completed his officer's training, and the following year, he graduated with a master's degree. In spite of his youth (he was only twenty-six years old at the time of the collision), *Stockholm*'s third mate had received a solid education and good practice at sea.

It was not surprising that Carstens was first employed at the Broström Group. As early as the turn of the twentieth century, this company had a leading position in the international shipping industry, and when Carstens began to look for a job, its ships were sailing almost everywhere on the Seven Seas.

During his training, Carstens had the advantage of sailing on several shipping routes. He sailed to the Mediterranean aboard Orient Line's *Sunnanland*. This route had been created in 1911 by Dan Broström of the second generation of the Broström dynasty, who had turned his attention to America. The result was Swedish America Mexico Line, whose shipping route Carstens was able to study on board *Trolleholm*.

East Asia had long been an area of great interest to Swedish trade and shipping. The various well-known and partially successful attempts at creating a permanent East India Company in the eighteenth century resulted in the establishment of the Swedish

East Asia Company, Inc., founded in 1907 by Dan Broström.

The company's first ship, *Canton,* was to have many successors whose names reflected the mysteriousness of the Orient. Such names as *Peking, Japan, Ceylon, Benares, Shantung, Mindoro, Mangalore, Trawancore, Minikoi,* and *Nagasaki* are bound to touch the hearts of many old seafarers. On board *Benares* and *Formosa,* Carstens had an opportunity to familiarize himself with this area of Swedish shipping and its proud traditions.

The Swedish East Asia Company was certainly one of the finest companies of the Broström Group. The traditions of the East India Company had to be lived up to, and the financial interests of the prominent Wallenberg family made the company even more prestigious. Being the president of this company was almost like being a member of the royal family. Therefore, it was natural that Dan-Axel, from the third generation of the Broström clan, took over in 1942 at the age of twenty-seven, after an interim "regency" following Dan Broström's death in 1925.

From July to September 1953, Carstens made a historic journey to China aboard Swedish East Asia Company's *Kinaland.* The ship was previously called *Formosa,* the former name of Taiwan, but it had to be renamed in order to call at a Chinese port. *Kinaland* was the first ship from a western country that was allowed to sail up the Yellow River after Mao seized power in 1949.

While Swedish America Line was the "jewel in the crown" to the general public, to the Broström family that honor belonged to Steamship Tirfing, Inc. The passenger ships of this company represented the dream of America in all respects.

The officers of the White Viking Fleet of Swedish America Line were selected from the most highly qualified of the Broström employees, unless they explicitly expressed a desire for calmer service on board the

In spite of his youth (he was only twenty-six years old), *Stockholm's* Third Mate Johan-Ernst Carstens-Johannsen had received a solid education, and he had good experience at sea.

cargo ships. After a few months as second mate on *Albatross,* the Broström Group's training ship to which only the best among the young officers in the company were assigned, Carstens was appointed third mate on *Kungsholm* in December 1955. *Kungsholm* had been delivered from Vlissingen in the Netherlands in 1953. In May 1956, Carstens came to *Stockholm.*

Thus, a highly qualified group of officers were standing on the bridge of *Stockholm* on the night of July 25 and 26. Carstens had an excellent education from two of Sweden's foremost naval and navigation colleges. Considering his age, his experience with different types of ships and shipping routes was extensive. While serving in the Swedish Navy, he had also been trained as a noncommissioned officer.

After his service aboard *Stockholm*, Carstens was transferred to *Gripsholm*, which had been built at the Ansaldo Shipyard in Genoa and delivered in 1957. He then served on various cargo ships, but in 1965, he went ashore for good. He was employed at the Broström Liner Agency, where his main responsibility was to buy equipment for the passenger ships. Until 1979, Carstens worked as manager of the Department for Equipment and Necessities within the Broström Trading Company. He was then transferred to Broström International Trading and made head of Broström Trading, Inc.

CHAPTER 4

A Perfectly Normal Day

July 25, 1956, was a perfectly normal summer day in New York City: oppressive heat combined with high humidity. A thick haze seemed to cover the city with a layer of moist dirt.

The inhabitants of the metropolis were very uncomfortable when they had to leave the pleasantly air-conditioned offices, department stores, and restaurants. Down by the docks along the Hudson River, a little cool air might be found, but not much. The big passenger ships lay anchored with their stems facing the Manhattan skyline, reminding people that it was still their era, and it was the height of the season for traveling to Europe and back.

The big ships arrived and departed like ferries. The arriving travelers had to be put ashore quickly in order to make room for new passengers. The docks—dark and dirty with awkwardly shaped buildings jutting out into the Hudson River—were a sharp contrast to the luxurious ships carrying all the travelers by sea to and from New York.

The ships were usually in port for a brief period of only two to three days, a hectic time when many tasks had to be done and nothing could be neglected. Everything had to be in place for a voyage across the Atlantic, where "the groceries weren't just around the corner."

On board Swedish America Line's *Stockholm,* which had been in port at Pier 97 for a couple of days, the routine was the same as the one carried out before every voyage. This consistency was necessary in order for the organization to function. What sometimes broke the standard pattern were messages from the office on shore about receptions, luncheons, or dinner parties for prominent guests, the press, or travel agents. These events were not very popular among the employees in the supply service on board, but they were probably necessary from a public relations point of view. The struggle for passengers and market share in the United States was extremely tough.

The crew had few opportunities to relax on shore during a brief stay in New York Harbor. The routine assignments did not allow much free time.

The day before *Stockholm's* departure on July 25, 1956, some of the crewmembers were given a few hours off duty. Carstens and his colleagues did not pass up this opportunity to visit the "old man in the wall," whose store was located just outside the dock area. Here one could purchase clothes, toiletries, and radio sets, to mention only a few of the hundreds of items that were for sale. It was a real general store offering a selection of products adapted to the needs of seafarers. It was part of an old tradition to visit the old man, and the prices he charged were very reasonable as well.

In small groups the crewmembers went to midtown Manhattan, where theaters, cinemas, restaurants, and bars were located close together. A visit to one of the "in" spots for seafarers was part of the routine for most of them, but it was important that they conduct themselves well. Discipline aboard *Stockholm* was strict, and being late back on the ship, or being drunk, would lead to punishment. In serious cases, a crewmember could even be discharged.

Consequently, a beer in a bar would usually be considered enough entertainment, or else a walk up to Times Square where Seventh Avenue intersects with Broadway. For those paying their first visit to New York, the excitement of life in the midtown area was a great experience.

Not many, not even the mates, went as far as the Fifth Avenue offices of Swedish America Line during the short stay of the ships. As a rule, it was only the commanding officers who made a courtesy call at the elegant premises on this fashionable street opposite St. Patrick's Cathedral.

The offices were located on two floors. On the ground floor was a reception desk and upstairs were the spacious offices. Along Fifth Avenue show windows featured models of the ships belonging to Swedish America Line. Information was provided on luxury cruises around the world or specialty cruises to the archipelagos of the South Seas.

Nothing could compare to the departure of a transatlantic liner in the heyday of passenger traffic in the 1950s. Very similar scenes were enacted in such ports as Gothenburg, Copenhagen, Oslo, Southampton, Amsterdam, Le Havre, Hamburg, Bremen, and Genoa. For a few hours, the pier and the ship formed a unit linked with gangways. To an outsider, it seemed like life in an anthill, with everybody moving in different directions. Passengers were having their luggage cleared by the customs officials; others were lining up for passport control or bidding farewell to those friends and acquaintances who were on the pier but had not obtained passes to go on board the ship. Porters authorized by the shipping company checked to see that all the luggage was delivered to the right cabins, and visitors with special passes sometimes seemed to inundate the departing ship. Amidst all this were flags, flowers, garlands, confetti, tears and laughter, joy and sorrow.

On board the ship, the hectic life continued. People found it difficult to make the most of the brief time allotted to them. In the lounges, cocktails were served in a steady stream at inexpensive, tax-free prices, and in the staterooms, bottles of champagne were uncorked. People were saying goodbye for a short time or forever. Would air traffic be able to create such a festive mood? Perhaps that attitude is part of the difference between traveling just for transport and traveling for personal enjoyment.

Such was the scene as *Stockholm* prepared for departure on July 25, 1956. At a signal, all the visitors were asked to leave the ship. A last toast, a last farewell, and then a general exodus from the ship. The dock seemed gloomy in comparison with the festive ship.

Everything happened so fast—perhaps too fast. At this stage, everything should have been in place and the ship ready to depart. As a floating hotel, it had been cleaned, packed with food supplies, and loaded with luggage and cars. All the instruments of the mechanical and navigational equipment had been carefully checked. The seaworthiness of the lifeboats also had been checked. In short, the ship was ready; all the crewmembers were at their stations.

A couple of tugboats were quickly at hand. The ship was unmoored. The last farewells were exchanged between the passengers and those left on the pier. Presently, *Stockholm* was in position midstream on the Hudson River. The ship's whistle sounded "Farewell New York."

At 1131 *Stockholm* was beginning her 103rd journey eastward. The great adventure was about to begin.

"A Holiday on the Atlantic Ocean" was to be the main slogan of Swedish America Line when traffic resumed at the end of World War II. The journeys were not only supposed to provide transportation between two continents, as in previous decades when air traffic offered no threat or competition, but also a unique opportunity for rest and relaxation.

Sailing was no longer "the only way to cross" but just one of two alternatives. Hence, it was crucial to convince people of the advantages of sea voyaging as compared to flying. A sea crossing was a means of transportation that had the stamp of tradition, an experience that the passengers would talk about for many years to come. Passengers should feel that they were following in the footsteps of other emigrants, immigrants, and settlers approaching their destination in an appropriate manner.

Naturally, the summer crossings were the most popular ones. It was easier for Swedish America Line's organization in the United States to sell Scandinavia as an attractive tourist destination in the summer. This was also the time of year when the awesome North Atlantic was usually in its very best mood.

It was just such a typical, summer crossing that *Stockholm* embarked upon from New York on July 25, 1956.

The legendary old passenger liner *Ile de France* had pulled out from one of the docks. Compared to the enormous hull of the liner, *Stockholm* almost looked like a coastal steamer. The two ships accompanied each other down the Hudson River, but when they passed the Statue of Liberty and *Ambrose* lightship, *Ile de France*, sailing at a speed of 23 knots as compared to *Stockholm*'s 18, gradually drew away and disappeared into the haze of the afternoon sun.

The harassed crew of a passenger liner usually enjoys leaving port and returning to their accustomed lives at sea. They begin to feel that they are at a safe distance from the offices on shore with their orders and counterorders. The exact departure time of *Stockholm* from New York was set at 1131. She carried 534 passengers, only 18 of whom were traveling first class. The number of crewmembers was 213.

During the departure from New York, all the officers were busy performing various tasks that had been assigned to them in advance. Captain Gunnar Nordenson was on the bridge when the pilot was discharged off Staten Island at 1332 (on the western side of the mouth of the Hudson River) and when the ship passed *Ambrose* lightship. After the captain had set the course at 90°, mainly following the shoreline of Long Island and heading for Nantucket, the standby was called off, and the ordinary watch took over.

To most of the passengers, the cruise had all the charm of novelty. They were looking forward to a pleasant, eight-day voyage across the North Atlantic. The crossing could hardly have gotten off to a better start. A cool breeze replaced the stifling heat of New York. A soft haze covered the horizon, and the ship moved along very gracefully in the long swell that constantly

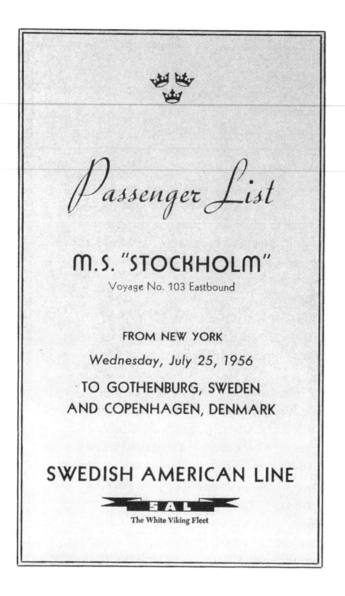

Passenger List

M.S. "STOCKHOLM"
Voyage No. 103 Eastbound

FROM NEW YORK

Wednesday, July 25, 1956

TO GOTHENBURG, SWEDEN
AND COPENHAGEN, DENMARK

SWEDISH AMERICAN LINE

SAL
The White Viking Fleet

SWEDISH AMERICAN LINE

M.S. STOCKHOLM

Commander
Captain G. NORDENSON

Chief Officer	H. Källback
Chief Engineer	G. Assargren
First Engineer	S. Boman
Chief Radio Officer	B. Mellgren
Chief Purser	C. Dawe
Cashier	T. Odenlund
Information Officer	Chris. Steman
Chief Steward	C. G. Quant
Ship's Doctor	Ā. Nessling

The cover of the passenger list from *Stockholm*'s 103rd voyage eastward from New York on July 25, 1956, and a list of the senior officers on board.

wanders across great oceans even in calm weather. There was no reason to switch on the stabilizers.

At lunch, directly after departure, the passengers had an opportunity to sample the famous cuisine of the ships of Swedish America Line. They then unpacked, went sightseeing to familiarize themselves with the various lounges on board, and went for a walk on deck, where the thermometer in-dicated 22° Celsius, comparable to the height of summer weather in Sweden.

Later in the afternoon, those who were so inclined could swim in the indoor pool, which had just been filled with crystal-clear, temperate water from the Atlantic. There was really nothing to mar this first day of the Atlantic crossing. A lifeboat drill had been scheduled for the following day, but other-wise, the program was not very demanding.

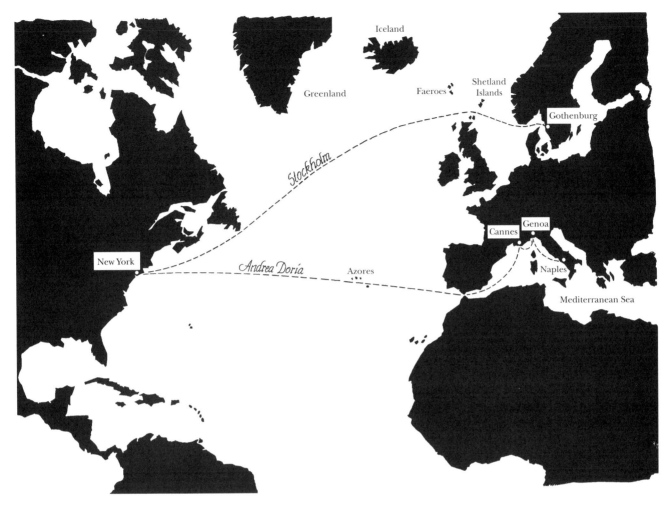

Iceland

Greenland

Faeroes

Shetland
Islands

Gothenburg

Stockholm

New York

Andrea Doria

Azores

Cannes Genoa

Naples

Mediterranean Sea

Andrea Doria departed from her home port, Genoa, on July 17, 1956. After calling at several Mediterranean ports, she sailed the "sunshine route" via the Azores. She was expected to arrive in New York on the morning of July 26.

 Stockholm departed from New York on July 25. After passing *Nantucket* lightship, she was to proceed on the markedly colder and rougher North Atlantic. Arrival at Gothenburg was to be on August 2 and at Copenhagen one day later.

The passengers were particularly looking forward to dinner, which was to be followed by dancing and a buffet at about 2300. But as pleasant as that all sounded, it was a long way off, and not everybody would have the energy for all that after such an eventful day. People needed to save their energy for the rest of the voyage. According to the timetable, *Stockholm* was to arrive on August 2 in Gothenburg and one day later in Copenhagen, where a festive reception would be waiting as usual.

Everything was expected to proceed according to the schedule.

CHAPTER 5

Heading for Nantucket:
"I See an Echo"

In 1956, *Ambrose* lightship marked the entrance to New York Harbor just as *Vinga* lightship was the first outpost for ships approaching Gothenburg. The sailing time, about two hours from lightship to dock, was also about the same.

At noon Junior Second Mate Sven Abenius had taken over the watch on the bridge, but Captain Nordenson also remained there until the pilot left the ship.

Normally, the warm New York weather would accompany the ships sailing along the shoreline of Long Island. *Stockholm* had no swimming pool on deck, but on the afternoon of July 25, she could have used one. The warm breeze and the sun, even though it was covered by some haze, combined to give an impression of summer in Sweden at its very best.

Later, on the voyage along the United States coast, the weather was expected to change. It was not unusual at this time of year for fog to appear in the area around Nantucket, where the cold winds and currents from the north met the warmer air masses and the Gulf Stream from the south.

Farther east, near Cape Race and southern Newfoundland, the temperature could get down almost to freezing, even in summer. Sometimes passengers on Swedish America Line's ships had the extraordinary experience of dancing on deck on a midsummer eve around a maypole decorated with flowers given to them on their departure from New York, and finding themselves in the middle of a light snowfall.

Stockholm still had a long way to go to Nantucket and Cape Race. The ship was moving gracefully in the light swell, and the passengers were taking leisurely walks or stretching out in the deck chairs they had rented for the entire crossing.

At 1511 Mate Abenius noted on the chart that the Fire Island buoy had been passed, which meant that *Stockholm* had sailed about half the length of the Long Island shoreline. *Ile de France* had long since disappeared in the heat haze on the horizon. At this time of day, traffic was quite light.

At 1600 it was time for the watch to be relieved again. Lars Eneström, who took over from Sven Abenius, continued to enjoy a very good day at sea. According to calculations, the course, which was still 90°, would take *Stockholm* about one nautical mile south of *Nantucket* lightship, but it might become necessary to correct the course later, since the currents were expected to drive the ship somewhat north.

At 1911 Mate Eneström noted having seen Block Island, which is located off the eastern tip of Long Island, on the radar. *Stockholm* was positioned 41 nautical miles from Block Island. Usually the island would not be spotted on the radar at a distance greater than 30 nautical miles. Consequently, Eneström noted on the chart: "Must have been a mirage. Warm air over colder water."

At 2030 it was time for Carstens to take over the watch on the bridge of *Stockholm*. Normally, this would have occurred at 2000, but since Carstens had earlier relieved Eneström on the bridge for a half-hour dinner break, his watch started later.

Eneström and Carstens were very good friends, and it was not unusual for the second mate, who was four years older, to remain on the bridge for some time to keep Carstens company. However, since the departure from New York had been strenuous, Eneström went down to his cabin after checking the course, position, and weather forecast as usual. Hence, from 2030 onward, Carstens was the only officer on the bridge of *Stockholm*.

What is it like to navigate at night? Does the watchstander tend to see things that do not exist?

Carstens explained:

I've heard about things like that, but I myself have never seen a "Flying Dutchman," nor have I experienced ghostlike mirages that have made me doubt that I was on the right course. As a matter of fact, it's easier to navigate at night than in daylight. Dusk is the most difficult time when you've got to pay extra attention. In a storm or in high seas, when you may think you see things that exist, or don't exist, you have to be on the alert. But I've never experienced any "hocus pocus."

Ten minutes after Carstens took over command on the bridge, Captain Nordenson came up to check on things. Just like the mate who had had the previous watch, he noticed that the current had taken *Stockholm* somewhat north, but still he adjusted the course an extra 3° to port to ensure a safe passage past *Nantucket* lightship. It was important to sail as near to it as possible, but without running a safety risk.

Nantucket would be *Stockholm*'s last fixed position on North America.

Would it have been safer to have two mates on the bridge?

Carstens replied:

That may be so, but I wasn't worried about being alone. It was in accordance with the international regulations at the time, and I'm not aware that it hasn't worked out satisfactorily at any time. On entering a harbor in narrow passages and in fog, either the captain or the chief mate would also be on the bridge.

Now that we were on our way to Nantucket, I also knew that Captain Nordenson would come up to the bridge well before the passage. It's true that I had a lot to do as the only mate on the bridge, but I didn't feel I was under stress in any way. Before I took over the watch, I had dinner and a nap, and I really felt bright-eyed and bushy-tailed.

And after all, I wasn't all alone. I was assisted by three sailors, who took turns as helmsman, lookout in the crow's nest, and as an extra lookout. The oldest of them, Peder Larsen, was twenty-six years old and not very familiar with *Stockholm*, since he had signed on eleven days earlier. Ingemar Björkman was twenty years old, and Sten Johansson only eighteen. Therefore, the safety of *Stockholm* was in the hands of us four youngsters, one of whom was still just a teenager.

A few months later, this fact was exploited to the limit by *Andrea Doria*'s owner, Italian Line, and by the lawyers who represented that shipping company.

What does a watchstander think about, knowing he is responsible for the safety of several hundred people on board a big passenger ship?

Carstens replied:

Nothing in particular. Everything is just a matter of routine, and not for a single moment did I imagine there might be an accident, least of all a collision. Everything on board a big ship with all the navigational equipment you can imagine has been planned in such great detail that only the "human element" remains, and that must function, of course.

My main responsibility during my first night watch on the bridge of *Stockholm* on her 103rd crossing eastward was to check carefully that everything functioned according to plan. The radar, which had been checked during our stay in New York, was found to function very well. The course set by Captain Nordenson was the normal one, and there was no more traffic than usual.

Sometimes you see ships, sometimes you don't. Distances are great, and it's rare that you catch sight of them; it's the radar that is our watchful eye. We had no information about ships departing from or arriving in New York, nor did we know anything about crossing traffic to Boston and Canadian ports, which was not unusual.

It had to be a game with unknown factors, a game we had played so many other times at sea. Yet, we were lucky compared to the ships of past times, because we had the radar, an instrument that could check many nautical miles around the ship.

Carstens continued:

In those days, it was very difficult to navigate along the shoreline of Long Island. It is a low coastline, and one must be constantly alert to check positions. In 1956 we didn't have navigation by satellite but only loran covering the American coastline and Decca covering the North Sea.

Among other things, it was part of the routine on the bridge to check the radar, the navigation lights, the lookout in the crow's nest, and the helmsman. There was really just one problem: Peder Larsen at the wheel. I noticed at an early stage that he was extremely interested in his surroundings and that he sometimes didn't pay full attention to the compass. I don't know if it was the beautiful moonlight or something else that made him absentminded, but I decided it would be necessary to keep an extra eye on him.

Another thing to worry about was our position in relation to the determined course. The radio bearings indicated that the currents had taken us between 2.5 and 3 nautical miles north, and I thought that was too much to allow us to pass *Nantucket* according to Captain Nordenson's instructions, i.e., about 1 nautical mile. At 2230 I therefore made a correction for 2° leeway. I didn't consider going further out from land. Of course, I knew about Track Charlie, a route ships headed for Europe could use, but Swedish America Line had never told us to use it. If Captain Nordenson, who was an extremely careful person and who kept track of all the instructions from shore, had been told that we were to sail 20 nautical miles further south, he would most certainly have done so.

Larsen, Björkman, and Johansson, the three men on the bridge, took turns performing different tasks according to a time schedule made up in advance. Hence, at 2240 Larsen took over the wheel from Johansson during the last hour of the watch, and Johansson climbed up to the crow's nest to be the lookout.

From this position, some 30 meters above sea level, he had a very clear bird's-eye view of everything that was moving in a wide circle around the ship. Ingemar Björkman, who had served as the lookout, was now allowed to go and rest in the standby's cabin, but he was summoned to the bridge every time I went into the chart room to determine our position.

The drift of *Stockholm* bothered me, and I found it difficult to cope with. When I determined our position again about a quarter of an hour after the latest correction, I found that the ship was still too far north, more precisely about 3 nautical miles. I then ordered another 2° starboard, and Larsen, the helmsman, turned the wheel to 91°. At the same time, I went over to the radar to make a routine check, and that's when I saw the echo of a ship—a small, pale green spot located somewhat on the port side of *Stockholm.*

This was nothing unusual in these waters; as a matter of fact, it was strange that there had been so little traffic that evening. It was still fair and warm; there was bright moonlight, and the ocean was almost calm. The passengers couldn't have had a better first day at sea, and some of them were still walking around on deck waiting for the night buffet to be served.

Every time you see an echo on the radar, it's important to have complete command of the situation. Was the approaching vessel a cargo or a passenger ship? There was also a possibility that it could be a warship or a large fishing boat, or it could be a slow ship that we were catching up with as we made 18 knots. And if it was a meeting vessel, what course was it on?

All these are things you know nothing about when you first see an echo at a substantial distance. But if you have access to a so-called plotting board and if you make a number of observations, you can get a clear idea of the situation pretty rapidly. By means of some simple calculations, you can establish the other vessel's speed and course. In other words, you can estimate (1) when you'll meet the unidentified ship, (2) if the two ships that will meet are on parallel courses, and (3) at what distance they may expect to pass each other.

That's exactly what I did. The radar observations soon indicated that it was a ship approaching at high speed. When I plotted again a short time later, I put a cross on the plotting board that showed that she was 2° on the port side of *Stockholm.* I also ordered Ingemar Björkman, the previous lookout in the crow's nest who was now resting, to be on the lookout from the port wing of the bridge.

When the unidentified ship was at a distance of 6 nautical miles, I plotted and found that it was at 4° off our port, i.e., left, side. At that very moment, Larsen struck six bells on the watch bell, which meant that it was 2300.

That latest plotting fully confirmed that *Stockholm* and the meeting ship were on parallel courses and that we'd pass each other at a distance between ½ a nautical mile and 1 nautical mile, i.e., about 1 kilometer.

It can be very difficult to explain to people who have no experience of navigating at sea what happens when two ships meet. Let me try to do it from a car driver's perspective.

Stockholm and the ship that would later turn out to be *Andrea Doria* were heading to and from New York on something like a multilane highway with a wide median strip separating the inbound and outbound lanes. This channel was estimated to be about 1 nautical mile wide, or the equivalent of 1,500 meters.

Since one keeps to the right at sea, just as on land, a vessel that's in danger of colliding or having a close encounter with an approaching ship should move to starboard, or to the right, just as we do on land. That's really all there is to it.

One of the first things I learned before going to sea was Article 18 of the International Rules of the Road at Sea, in effect from 1897 to 1977. It read as follows:

> When two steam vessels are meeting end on, or nearly end on so as to involve risk of collision, each shall alter her course to starboard so that each shall pass on the port side of the other. [The 1972 international rules went into effect on July 15, 1977.]

It was Captain Nordenson's standing order that there should be at least 1 nautical mile between *Stockholm* and an approaching ship. It would therefore be necessary to correct *Stockholm*'s course again, but this should preferably not be done until the other ship had been sighted visually, and it was possible to see its top lights and use them to determine its position.

Strangely enough, we couldn't see any lights from the oncoming ship, although it was only 4 nautical miles away. By now I had adjusted the radar to the immediate radius of 5 nautical miles. The echo had grown larger, and all three of us—myself, Björkman on the bridge, and Johansson in the crow's nest—were gazing out across a dark ocean where we could still not see any lights even though visibility was good. It was strange but hardly alarming.

So far, it had been a perfectly normal day on the Atlantic Ocean.

CHAPTER 6

Andrea Doria Encounters Fog

Italian Line had a distinct advantage over Swedish America Line. Almost all year long, her ships could begin their voyages to the United States under pleasant weather conditions. For Swedish America Line's ships, even during the summer months, the North Sea and its troubled waters could constitute a trial.

The first three or four days in the Mediterranean after departure from Genoa, Italian Line's home port, could almost be described as a "mini cruise." The calls at Cannes on the French Riviera, Naples, and Gibraltar made the trip varied and rich in experiences right from the start.

Andrea Doria had left Genoa on July 17, 1956, on her fifty-first and, as it would turn out, her last voyage. Later, her passengers and the Italian newspapers called attention to the fact that in Italy the number seventeen is regarded as unlucky, like the number thirteen in some other countries.

As she steamed out onto the North Atlantic on July 20, *Andrea Doria* had 1,134 passengers on board, the majority, 677, in third class. Unlike *Stockholm, Andrea Doria* had three classes: first, cabin, and tourist, also referred to as first, second, and third class.

As so many times in the past, the ship was fully booked. Many people had been on the standby list but had not managed to get places. The maximum cabin capacity was 1,221, but it was rare that any passenger liner reached its maximum because some double cabins were occasionally sold to a single person, and some cabins designed for four people were assigned to only two.

Among *Andrea Doria*'s passengers were many emigrants who, in possession of immigration visas, were seeking their fortunes on the other side of the Atlantic. To assist them, the head of Italian emigration, Naval Lieutenant Commander Giuseppe Campo, was also on board.

For the most part, *Andrea Doria*'s fifty-first trip from Genoa to New York resembled all her previous crossings. After a few days, the passengers had settled into the rhythm of life on board and made themselves at home in the ship's lounges. On *Andrea Doria*, as on all other Atlantic liners, there was a distinct segregation of classes. For example, no one in third class could visit relatives or friends in another class without permission.

Yet, *Andrea Doria* was nonetheless a dream for all her guests. Although the ship had not been built as a "one class" vessel, her standards were high when compared to ships built before World War I, especially with respect to third class.

Of course, the cabins were not large, and with berths for four people, it could feel claustrophobic without access to any daylight through portholes. But that was not a major problem—after all, guests were normally in their cabins only when they wanted to sleep.

The passengers who lived farthest down on B and C decks, especially in the forward part of *Andrea Doria,* were not totally comfortable. Some cabins were even located all the way up in the forepeak. When the wind freshened and *Andrea Doria* heaved in high seas, it was like riding up and down on an express elevator at dizzying speed.

Under such circumstances, it was best for the well-being of the passengers to stay in the lounge around the clock. Many travel accounts—including some written after *Andrea Doria* went down—praised the wonderful life on board and all the efforts made by the personnel to ensure that the passengers would have a good time. The Italian cuisine—both the food and the wines—and the consistently attentive crew meant that even the poorest emigrants could feel like first-class passengers during the journey of more than a week across the Mediterranean and Atlantic to the United States.

The many lounges with comfortable furniture and exquisite artwork attracted people virtually around the clock. Dancing, entertainment, movies, and cocktail parties ensured that no one had to worry about how to pass the time.

On deck rich opportunities for relaxation could be found. Skeet shooting and shuffleboard were always on the program, and three swimming pools were available to passengers in all classes. The pools were surrounded by spacious decks where the passengers could eat, drink, and sun themselves. To stroll about leisurely on *Andrea Doria*'s Lido Deck was almost like being at a luxury hotel on the Mediterranean seashore.

An ocean voyage across the Atlantic has many highlights, esteemed in varying degrees by different passengers. No voyage is like any other. The temperature and the winds change with the seasons. On every voyage, however, there are two fixed details on the program, which everyone normally remembers: the lifeboat drill and the farewell dinner. Laws and regulations of the sea mandate the former; the latter has become a tradition that only the most terrible weather could cancel.

The purpose of the lifeboat drill is for everybody on board, passengers and crew alike, to know where they are to be if the worst happens. It might seem as though the lifeboat drills are unnecessary on ships equipped with modern technology and provided with watertight bulkheads that theoretically make them unsinkable. By 1956 it might also have seemed that there was another good reason to cancel this rather old–fashioned tradition: viewed statistically, it was entirely uncalled-for.

The Transatlantic Passenger Conference founded in 1919 by the shipping companies that trafficked the North Atlantic could present statistics showing that not one person had died or been severely injured on a passenger ship since World War I because the ship sank. This was remarkable because between 1919 and 1956, no fewer than 27 million people had been transported across the Atlantic.

Considering the improvements in maritime safety facilities, it appeared that the likelihood of a major catastrophe at sea was virtually nil. Perhaps it was not so strange that the crew of the unsinkable *Andrea Doria* was rather relaxed about the lifeboat drill on July 18 as the ship was heading from Naples to Gibraltar.

On that day, whistles and loudspeakers urged all the people on board to take their life jackets and report immediately to the lifeboat stations, where they were to receive further instructions. The passengers were quickly in place, but no crewmembers were visible. After waiting a long time, the people assumed that the drill was over and dispersed.

"Maybe we don't need any instructions," someone suggested. "After all, *Andrea Doria* can't sink anyway."

Traditionally, the farewell dinner on passenger liners destined for New York took place on the evening before arrival, celebrating the end of a successful crossing. But when it was estimated that arrival would occur very early in the morning, it seemed appropriate to move this great party forward one day. *Andrea Doria* was expected in New York between 0600 and 0700 on July 26, so Captain Calamai decided to have the farewell dinner one day earlier, on July 24 rather than July 25.

He had good reason to suspect that a party on the night before arriving in New York would be a bit of a failure, since the passengers would be going ashore so early the next morning. The dinner was precisely as festive as everyone had hoped. Kitchen and dining room personnel made every effort to surpass their usual fine performance, and Captain Calamai, who had no great appetite for social occasions, somewhat reluctantly turned up.

That very evening, however, he had reason to show himself only sporadically in the lounges. The wind had picked up, and the now top-heavy *Andrea Doria* was rolling in the heavy seas. There was no cause for anxiety just then. It was not the hard weather that primarily concerned Captain Calamai; rather, it was the massive fogbank that could stretch from the area around Nantucket for

CABIN CLASS

NO MORE CHANGING OF TIME

Wednesday
25
JULY 1956

From 7 to 8:30 a.m.	HOLY MASSES in the Chapel
From 7:30 - 9:30 am	BREAKFAST
At 9:00 a.m.	PHYSICAL CULTURE CLASS in the Gymnasium
At 10:00 a.m.	DECK-GAMES (Please see the Deck-Steward)
At 10 - 11:00 a.m.	BROADCAST MUSIC
At 11:00 a.m.	TRAP SHOOTING (Weather permitting)
At 11:45 a.m.	LUNCHEON — (First Sitting)
At 1:15 p.m.	LUNCHEON — (Second Sitting)
At 1:45 p.m.	MOVIES in the Ball Room

Featuring:
La fortuna di essere donna   Comedy in Italian
Sophia Loren, Marcello Mastroianni, Elisa Cegani, Charles Boyer

At 3:30 p.m.	CONCERT in the Ball Room
At 4:00 p.m.	TEA in the Lounge
At 4:45 p.m.	MOVIES in the Ball Room

Featuring:
« FOX FIRE »   Drama in English
Jeff Chandler, Jane Russell

At 6:45 p.m.	DINNER — (First Sitting)
At 8:15 p.m.	DINNER — (Second Sitting)
At 9:30 p.m.	BINGO in the Ball Room
At 10:15 p.m.	DANCING IN THE BALL ROOM
At 11:30 p.m.	COLD BUFFET in the Grand Bar
At 12:00 mid-night	NIGHT CLUB IN THE VERANDA

Passengers are requested to have their baggage ready to-day at 3:30 p.m.

At that time the cabin Personnel will begin the transportation of the baggage from the cabins to the Promenade Deck to facilitate disembarkation.
To-morrow Passengers will find their baggage on the Pier, under the initial of their names. We warn Passengers not to leave personal documents, required for their landing, in the baggage.

Bank Office will be opened from 10:00 to 11.00 a.m. It will be closed in the afternoon.

Passengers are kindly requested, upon arrival at the Pier, not to gather on the enclosed promenade decks in order not to interfere with the landing of their baggage. In their own interest, we advise them also to leave the Ship after the disembarkation of the baggage. This will avoid a long wait on the Pier.

Andrea Doria's program for the day before arrival in New York. Chief Purser Curt Dawe found this together with other material on *Stockholm's* foredeck after the collision. The program had landed there as a result of the collision.

hundreds of nautical miles to the south at that time of year.

But that was still a long way off, and all the passengers who had learned to deal with *Andrea Doria's* rolling, pitching, and swaying passage through the waves would be celebrating in the ballrooms far into the night, a premature finale to a thus-far happy voyage.

On the morning of July 25, as *Andrea Doria* began her last day's voyage before arriving in New York, the sky was almost perfectly clear, and it was still pleasantly warm. Despite the lovely weather, there was something of a "day-after" mood on board. The festive, eight-day crossing was now as good as over, and everyday life was approaching. For many people a whole new life was about to begin in an entirely different environment and largely among strangers. What surprises would the New World have in store for all the immigrants?

For everyone on board, this was the day to start packing. Some passengers might also find time for a private farewell party with old or new friends before the day drew to a close.

The printed program for the day advised the passengers to have their luggage ready by 1530, when it would be transported up onto the promenade deck. On the following day, July 26, it would be in safekeeping and ready to be picked up on the pier in New York, organized by the passengers' last initials: that's the way it had always been done, and that's the way it would be this time.

Still, there was almost an entire day remaining before arrival in New York, and, of course, it had to be used for something other than packing. Those who were early risers could take the opportunity to attend Mass, which was held in the beautiful chapel on the foyer deck from 0700 to 0830. After breakfast those who felt like it could take part in deck games and skeet shooting, weather permitting, and it did so permit on this lovely and warm final day at sea.

Lunch could be enjoyed either in the dining rooms or at one of the buffets available at the pools on deck. After that an Italian comedy would be shown with Sophia Loren and Charles Boyer in the leading roles. Then two viewings of *Foxfire* would be offered later in the afternoon and evening before it was time for the last dinner, followed by bingo and dancing in the ballroom starting at 2215. Two additional items were on the program of this fantastic voyage for those who were still hungry and looking for entertainment: the cold buffet at 2330 and the nightclub that opened at midnight. Such was the program, and the pleasure seekers expected the schedule to be just as planned.

At around 1500 on July 25, fog began spreading all around *Andrea Doria*—not thick and impenetrable, but light and sporadic. The ship was heading straight for *Nantucket* lightship, still 160 nautical miles away.

Robert Young, Chief Inspector of the western European section of the Bureau of Shipping, had eaten lunch at the buffet of one of the first-class swimming pools and could confirm that the temperature was pleasant, even though the distant haze hinted that fog was approaching. Later in the afternoon, he noted to his horror that a cargo ship had suddenly crossed *Andrea Doria*'s course directly behind her. No one had seen it earlier.

Young, who was an expert at classifying the seaworthiness of ships, observed that *Andrea Doria* was top-heavy, and he judged that it would be difficult to restore stability if she should be subjected to some external influence. However, this was only an intellectual hypothesis that would surely not occur in reality.

Even if something should occur despite all her navigation and safety features, *Andrea Doria* was well equipped to save everyone on board. Unlike *Titanic,* which had a lifeboat capacity for only 1,178 people even though she had 2,207 on board, the lifeboats of *Andrea Doria* could accommodate 2,000 people. That was quite satisfactory, since she carried a total of only 1,708 people, including passengers and crew.

Captain Calamai was said to have been provided with a special alarm system for use when his ship was expected to enter a foggy area. Even before the alarm was sounded, the captain would be on the bridge, prepared to stay there as long as visibility was reduced.

For Captain Calamai, the fog on the afternoon of July 25 was not unexpected. It was actually the rule rather than the exception in this area that suddenly, after a sunny day, the ship would find itself in an impenetrable shroud.

There was no sign of improvisation in the measures taken by the captain under the prevailing circumstances. The actions were well known and often rehearsed on many similar occasions. Captain Calamai did not really need to give any specific orders. Everyone on the bridge knew that the two radar installations had to be observed with extra attention, that the ship's foghorn must be turned on, that the watertight doors must be closed, that the mast lookout should move all the way forward, and that engine room personnel should be informed of the risk of fog.

All of these measures were carried out in peace and quiet in accordance with the captain's orders. The fog thickened during the afternoon. Sometimes it was so thick that people on the bridge could not see the ship's stem.

Every passenger liner is required to stay strictly on schedule, and any captain who cannot show due cause for reducing speed can expect a reprimand from his company. Any delay implies not only increased fuel costs, but also extra harbor fees for personnel who have been ordered on standby duty for longer or shorter periods of time.

Actually, *Andrea Doria* would have been forced to lie almost perfectly still if Captain Calamai had applied a strict interpretation of the International Regulations for Preventing Collisions at Sea which were in effect at the time of the *Stockholm–Andrea Doria* collision:

> Rule 16. Speed in Fog. Every vessel shall, in a fog, mist, falling snow, or heavy rain storms, go at a moderate speed, having careful regard to the existing circumstances and conditions.
>
> A steam vessel hearing apparently forward of her beam the fog signal of a vessel the position of which is not ascertained shall, so far as the circumstances of the case admit, stop her engines, and then navigate with caution until danger of collision is over.

The expression "moderate speed" has been interpreted in different ways according to the existing circumstances but has generally been taken to mean that a ship should be able to stop within half the visible distance. The distance from the bridge of *Andrea Doria* to the forepeak where the lookout was posted, which could hardly be made out because of the fog, was about 60 meters.

This implies that the Italian vessel would have been practically lying still in the water if she had observed the existing rules. Possibly, she might have maintained steerageway to avoid drifting around uncontrolled.

However, rules and regulations were one thing, reality another. There was probably not a sea captain in the world who followed the regulations all the time. Had he done so in every situation, he would presumably not have grown old in his appointment. With too many schedule delays, he would simply have been too expensive for his employer.

Therefore, nobody could have seriously blamed Captain Calamai for reducing *Andrea Doria*'s speed only a small amount, from 23 to 21.8 knots. With all the navigational equipment Calamai had at his disposal on the bridge, he accepted the calculated risk that his company required.

Yet, the captain also had overall responsibility for the ship and everyone on board.

As long as no accident occurred when a ship traveled at full speed through dense fog, the captain was lauded as bold and dependable. But should a catastrophe occur, he alone had to bear the entire blame.

Captain Calamai was a captain who stubbornly refused to leave his ship's bridge when the fog was thick. During the afternoon of July 25, he made only two brief visits to his cabin when visibility improved a bit. In the evening he exchanged his white summer uniform for the blue one he used the rest of the year. A navy blue beret would protect his rather bald pate from the chilly damp air that accompanied the fog.

When it was time to relieve the watch at 2000, the fog was still thick. At best, visibility was limited to half a nautical mile, but still the ship raced ahead in a shroud of mist that made it impossible to see either the bow or the stern from the wings of the bridge.

Andrea Doria normally had two mates on the bridge, and relieving the watch always followed a schedule drawn up beforehand. First Mate Luigi Oneto, who was the highest ranking officer on the deck, now turned the bridge over to Second Mate Curzio Franchini, while Third Mate Eugenio Giannini relieved Assistant Mate Guido Badano. In addition to the two mates, Captain Calamai was also on the bridge, and everyone expected that he would remain there all night if the fog did not let up.

Mate Badano, checking the radar, observed that three ships were in the vicinity of *Andrea Doria*—one to starboard, one to port, and one off her stern. In contrast to the practice on *Stockholm,* the commanders of *Andrea Doria* did not use plotting but only estimated the approximate course and speed of other vessels by trying to remember how the echo on the radar screen shifted positions from time to time. This procedure would be the subject of much discussion later on.

Around 2100 a light was seen in the middle of the radar screen directly on *Andrea Doria*'s course. It was *Nantucket* lightship, and it was expected to show there. The course—267°—headed straight toward the lightship, which would have been cut in half without a change in course. At a distance of 17 nautical miles from the lightship, Captain Calamai gave the order to steer 261°, quite in accordance with earlier routines on voyages to New York.

They passed *Nantucket* at 2220 at an estimated distance of 1 nautical mile, and the course was set at 268°. This would head *Andrea Doria* directly toward *Ambrose* lightship outside the entrance to New York.

Thus far everything had proceeded exactly according to plan, but suddenly something vague and indistinct showed up on *Andrea Doria*'s radar screen: a little dot on the outermost edge of the screen. Mate Franchini, who had relieved the tired radar crewman, thought at first it was a small, slow-moving ship that *Andrea Doria* was catching up to, but he soon noticed it was an oncoming vessel.

The first radar contact *Andrea Doria* had with the ship that would later prove to be Swedish America Line's *Stockholm* was at a distance of 17 nautical miles. The officers on the bridge estimated her relative position to be 4° to starboard. The officers felt no cause to be uneasy. It was quite normal to both meet and overtake other ships in this heavily trafficked thoroughfare between Nantucket and New York. The ocean was big, and there was no reason to anticipate difficulties in passing at a safe distance.

When the two ships were at a distance of about 7 nautical miles, *Andrea Doria*'s radar was switched to a measuring range of 8 nautical miles. Now the echo doubled in size, but neither Captain Calamai nor his mates saw any reason to change course because, according to their interpretation, the vessels would pass each other at a distance of about 1 nautical mile.

At a distance of 5 nautical miles according to Captain Calamai (3½ according to Mate Franchini) the captain decided it would be safest to change *Andrea Doria*'s course 4° to port. That was the first measure taken since the other ship had been detected.

What was it that lay hidden beyond the fog barrier? Since no plotting had been done, only a qualified guess was possible about the oncoming ship's course and speed. And how would the two vessels pass? The officers on the bridge decided on starboard-to-starboard, but now the moment of truth was at hand.

CHAPTER 7

A Collision in a Display of Sparks

As *Andrea Doria* was swiftly approaching the unidentified ship, the crew on the bridge was growing seriously worried. Suddenly, the wide ocean with its almost unlimited possibilities to give way had been reduced to the Long Island Expressway, where any navigational error could end in disaster.

Captain Calamai was fully aware of this as he stood on the dark bridge gazing out into the dense fog. It was true that he had not plotted the other ship's course, but once he had decided that the meeting ship would pass on *Andrea Doria*'s starboard side, he really could not make any changes in the situation. The next few minutes would tell whether his assessment was correct.

As far as holding the farewell dinner one day earlier, Captain Calamai had made the right decision. It would most likely have been a rather tame party if it had been given the evening before arrival in New York. As early as 2200, the number of passengers in *Andrea Doria*'s lounges was diminishing, but those who wanted to have a good time were dancing as usual and would probably continue to do so until well into the wee hours.

In the Belvedere Lounge, located on the deck above the captain's bridge and the favorite place of the first-class passengers, another request had just been made for "Arrivederci Roma" ("Farewell to Rome"), that year's most popular song in Italy. In the second-class ballroom, too, people were dancing to a professional band, while the third-class passengers had to make do with the music played by an amateur band made up of members of the crew.

At this moment, a couple of minutes past eleven, nobody knew that *Andrea Doria* was sailing into a dramatic close encounter with another ship. Neither did they know that it would be a matter of life or death for some of the passengers whether they were in their cabins or had chosen to stay up and have a good time.

For Captain Calamai, it was a mystery that he and his officers on the bridge had no visual contact with the approaching ship now that the distance between them had shrunk to less than 2 nautical miles (about 3 kilometers). Despite the miserable visibility, *Andrea Doria* was still steaming at a speed of 21.8 knots.

Then, suddenly, it happened: "There she is," shouted Third Mate Eugenio Giannini, who was standing on the wing of the bridge peering intently into the fog. The light was weak, just barely perceptible, but Captain Calamai agreed that he, too, had seen something gleam. At the same time, the lookout, who was still standing on the bow of *Andrea Doria*, called the bridge and reported seeing lanterns (a ship's navigation lights) to starboard.

Now that people on *Andrea Doria* had caught sight, however dim, of the oncoming ship, Second Mate Curzio Franchini left his post at the radar screen and joined the others on the wing of the bridge. He gathered from the conversation between the captain and the third mate that they were observing the approaching ship, but in reality, at that moment, all they had seen were some very uncertain gleams of light.

Mate Giannini, who had never previously stood on the bridge of *Andrea Doria* in foggy conditions, was the first to see the oncoming vessel's lights. At first he sized up their relative positions—the forward white masthead light was visible to the right of the aft light—as if the two ships' courses were parallel and the approaching ship was on the starboard side of *Andrea Doria*.

But in the next moment, when visibility had further improved, everything was different. Now he clearly saw that the lower, forward masthead light was to the left of the aft light, and he also saw the other ship's red port light. That was a fearsome discovery: *Andrea Doria* was not going to pass the other ship starboard-to-starboard!

Now Captain Calamai was faced with the most difficult decision of his life. In which direction should he turn? Until now, he had thought that the oncoming ship was on his starboard side, so he had corrected his course to port. Yet, despite that, he found himself now on a collision course. To avoid

a catastrophe, he had to choose among four alternatives in principle: (1) swerve to starboard, (2) swerve to port, (3) proceed on the course already set, or (4) order full stop and reverse engines. He chose hard to port at practically full speed.

The second mate rushed to the engine room telegraph to stop engines, but Captain Calamai shouted, "Leave the engines alone; she'll turn faster!" He hoped that through his quick maneuver, *Andrea Doria* would manage to pass in front of the ship that was now on her starboard side or that they would slide close by one another.

Had Captain Calamai ordered full stop and reverse, the speed of *Andrea Doria* would not have been reduced much, as she had a braking distance of 3 nautical miles, due to the low reversing effect of turbine engines as compared with that of diesel engines.

In any case, there would have been an even worse catastrophe, not only for *Andrea Doria,* but also for the oncoming ship. There is much to suggest that Captain Calamai's decision not to order "stop and reverse" prevented *Andrea Doria* from cutting *Stockholm* in half.

A ship weighing 29,100 tons does not turn the way a car does. Hence, *Andrea Doria* was carried by her own momentum several hundred meters straight ahead, even though her rudder lay hard to port. But when she did begin to turn, another force of nature took hold: the circle grew tighter as she leaned to starboard.

On the bridge, the helmsman lay all his weight on the wheel—as though he could will *Andrea Doria* to move even faster to port. Captain Calamai stood at the rail and awaited the inevitable. When he saw the contours and then the bow of the oncoming ship, he instinctively flinched.

In the first-class Belvedere Lounge, the popular tune of "Arrivederci Roma" came to an abrupt end when the members of the

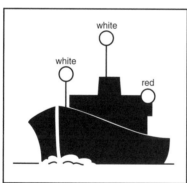

white

white

red

The artist has tried to reconstruct the situation on *Stockholm* when Mate Carstens-Johannsen and the two lookouts—one on the port bridge wing, the other in the crow's nest—saw the lights of *Andrea Doria* for the first time at a distance of about 1.8 nautical miles. Carstens was at the radar when he saw three lights. The lower, forward masthead light was clearly visible to the left of the higher, aft masthead light. He also saw the red port light of the approaching ship. At that time, everything indicated that the vessels would pass one another with a good margin, but to ensure that the ships would pass at a safe distance of at least one nautical mile, Carstens ordered a 20° starboard turn.

OUT OF THE FOG

band and their instruments fell off the band-stand. The dancing couples fell over. The liquor bottles in the bar were smashed to pieces.

Dancing in the second-class ballroom also came to an abrupt end. There too, "Arrivederci Roma" had been requested for the third or fourth time when chairs and tables were suddenly torn loose and dancing couples and waiters were thrown around the room. There was chaos as the lights went out, and everybody rushed for the exits.

In the third-class dining room, where a movie was just being shown, panic broke out. People almost trampled each other in their attempts to get out on deck or to their cabins in order to find life vests.

Scared and confused people, all wondering what had happened, appeared from bars, gambling parlors, and reading rooms. Was it a mine or a submarine, or was it perhaps one of the steam boilers that had exploded?

The questions asked by all these confused people were not answered. There were not many eyewitnesses to the collision, and information on board *Andrea Doria* was extremely scarce, almost nonexistent. Only a few people knew that the ship had quickly begun to heel over and assume a list that was to seal her fate.

On the bridge of *Stockholm,* Johan-Ernst Carstens-Johannsen was stunned. To him, the maneuvers of *Andrea Doria* were incomprehensible.

Carstens related:

When the echo on the radar screen was 2 nautical miles away, or perhaps somewhat less, the thing that we had been waiting for so intensely on the bridge and in the crow's nest actually happened. Ingemar Björkman, who was on the port wing of the bridge of *Stockholm,* suddenly shouted, "Lanterns to port!" He also reported seeing a weak, red

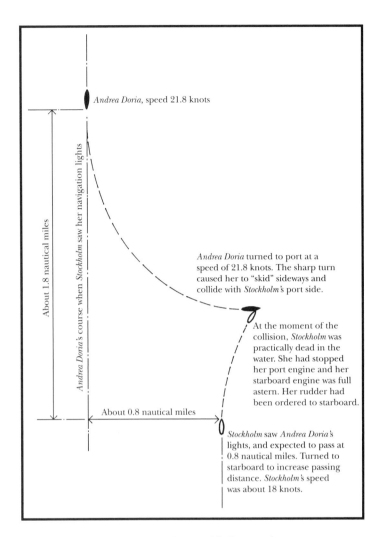

Andrea Doria, speed 21.8 knots

Andrea Doria turned to port at a speed of 21.8 knots. The sharp turn caused her to "skid" sideways and collide with *Stockholm'*s port side.

At the moment of the collision, *Stockholm* was practically dead in the water. She had stopped her port engine and her starboard engine was full astern. Her rudder had been ordered to starboard.

Stockholm saw *Andrea Doria'*s lights, and expected to pass at 0.8 nautical miles. Turned to starboard to increase passing distance. *Stockholm'*s speed was about 18 knots.

About 1.8 nautical miles

*Andrea Doria'*s course when *Stockholm* saw her navigation lights

About 0.8 nautical miles

This sketch was made in accordance with Carstens's instructions to illustrate how the third mate saw the situation from the time *Andrea Doria* became visible until the moment of collision.

light, which indicated that he also observed the port lantern of the approaching ship.

I made the same observation at the radar equipment and, binoculars in hand, joined Björkman on the wing of the bridge. There was no doubt whatsoever: we were meeting a ship which we would admittedly pass at a distance of less than 1 nautical mile but which was distinctly on the port side of *Stockholm.* The red port lantern as well as the top lanterns, the lower one at the stem to the left of the one at the stern — nothing contradicted the calculations I had made by plotting. All the odds were in favor of a safe passing.

But since I had a standing order from Captain Nordenson that we shouldn't meet another ship at a distance of less than 1 nautical mile, I decided to turn 20° to starboard in order to guarantee that distance. *Stockholm* answered the helm quickly, and it wasn't many seconds before she was on her new course.

Then the phone rang on the bridge. It was Sten Johansson, the lookout in the crow's nest, who reported that the lights from the approaching ship were about 20° to port—a perfectly normal observation after the change of course I'd just ordered.

Then something I could never have imagined happened. The lookout in the crow's nest, the man on the port wing of the bridge, and I all simultaneously observed a drastic change of course in what would turn out to be *Andrea Doria*. We saw it in the top lanterns which quickly changed positions. The lower one at the stem was now markedly to the right of the higher one aft, and in addition, the green starboard lantern was now clearly visible.

I immediately understood that we were approaching a catastrophe. *Andrea Doria* had left her "right lane" on her way to the *Ambrose* lightship and New York and was crossing the "median strip."

In a last desperate attempt to avoid disaster, I gave orders that the helmsman should steer hard to starboard and that the engines should be stopped and then set to full-speed astern. I also had the watertight doors closed. *Stockholm* was now swiftly veering to starboard, and the crew in the engine room was working full speed. The entire ship shook as the braking effect took hold.

After making all the maneuvers possible to avoid an accident, I went out to the far end of the port wing and waited. *Andrea Doria* was now approaching us diagonally from behind, and since *Stockholm* was sailing at a considerably reduced speed, it was impossible for us to get away.

Carstens continued:

As I said before, I'd never seen a "Flying Dutchman" or experienced ghostlike mirages at sea, but to me, *Andrea Doria* became such a "ghost ship" when she turned up all of a sudden and without reason not in front of me, but beside me. She materialized dramatically before my very eyes as a gigantic ship, as an enormous floating hotel with light streaming out of portholes and festively lighted lounges.

And then the unavoidable happened: the crash, the shower of sparks as iron ground into iron; fireworks illuminating the dark ocean. I didn't experience the actual collision so much like two speeding cars crashing into each other but slower and heavier, more like a knife cutting through butter. But the crash, the din, and the light effects gave us an idea of the violent forces that had been unleashed.

It was a strange and frightening experience. A short while ago, I had seen an echo on the radar screen indicating a vessel to the left of our direction of travel. Now I was suddenly standing 12 meters from one of the world's most luxurious passenger liners—*Andrea Doria*.

From my position on the bridge of *Stockholm,* I could look straight into the dark bridge of *Andrea Doria*. I saw people moving around quickly, but I couldn't spot the captain of the ship. I never heard any moaning or calls for help. Of course I should have, but all the sounds made by humans were drowned out by the crashes as the strong plating gave way and as steel beams were broken like matches. It all happened very quickly. I don't think anyone timed it, but it probably didn't take more than a few seconds from the collision itself until *Andrea Doria* proceeded ahead of us at full speed.

Ordinary Seaman Sten Johansson, who was later called "a very valuable witness" by Swedish America Line at the preliminary hearing in New York, had had a bird's-eye view of the collision from *Stockholm*'s crow's nest. This is what he had to say about those dramatic minutes:

Due to the wind created by the speed of the ship, it was always cold in the crow's nest, even on warm summer evenings, and so we often smuggled a blanket from the passengers' deck chairs up there.

The most striking thing about that particular evening was the beautiful moonlight,

Immediately after the collision, *Andrea Doria*'s momentum carried her about a mile beyond the site, but then the current carried her back toward *Stockholm*, and she passed at a distance of only 500 meters. She was already listing 18° to starboard.

and the view was really perfect. From my high position, it wasn't any problem for me to detect oncoming ships and to estimate their course by means of the position of the navigation lights and the color of the side lanterns.

My first contact with the ship that would turn out to be *Andrea Doria* occurred when I spotted her top lanterns at a distance of about 2 nautical miles. The lower one at the stem was distinctly to the left of the higher one at the stern. By using the protractor available in the crow's nest, I estimated the angle to be 20°, and my observations were confirmed by reports from the bridge.

Nothing at all seemed alarming, but suddenly I was horrified to see the top lanterns change positions and the ship veer sharply toward us at the same time as *Stockholm* moved to starboard. After that, every-

thing happened very fast. The two distant lights turned out to belong to an enormous passenger liner that was now turning her entire illuminated broadside towards us.

Then there was a crash; a shower of sparks lit up the night sky. I was standing high up there in the unprotected crow's nest when the mast swung violently. I got down on deck as quickly as I could. At that very moment, I couldn't grasp that I had been a witness—maybe from the best vantage point imaginable—to the most famous collision in the history of shipping.

My fear soon died away as I was given new tasks. First of all, I was instructed to check that all portholes were closed, and then I was to be in command of one of the manually operated lifeboats that were sent over to *Andrea Doria*. It was a terrifying experience to see the situation close at hand and to see all those people in distress waiting for help.

What surprised me most was that all the portholes of *Andrea Doria* were open which must also have contributed to flooding the entire ship with water.

Andrea Doria was lying still at a distance of about 1 nautical mile from *Stockholm*. All her lights were on, and two red lanterns had been hoisted behind the wheelhouse to signal that the ship could not be maneuvered. The foghorns were sounding incessantly.

The collision had disastrous results, since seven of *Andrea Doria's* eleven decks had been torn open. According to stability calculations, *Andrea Doria* would not heel over more than 15°, but now she quickly heeled over 18, 19, and 20° in a few minutes. Several hundred tons of seawater flooded the empty starboard tanks, and since the port tanks were also nearly empty, the result became much more serious than it would have been otherwise.

Most of the water rushed into the generator room, thereby sealing the fate of *Andrea Doria* in just a few minutes.

The SOS message from *Andrea Doria* in her position—40°30'N, 69°53'W—triggered one of the greatest sea rescue operations in peacetime. The freighter *Cape Ann* was the first to arrive at the scene, followed by the transport vessel *Thomas* and, at about 0200, *Ile de France*, which had interrupted her voyage after some hesitation. The rescue station in New York alerted the Third Coast Guard District which sent out salvage vessels from several different ports to assist *Andrea Doria*.

CHAPTER 8

Is *Stockholm* Going Down?

An outsider cannot even begin to imagine the confusion that arose on the captain's bridge after the two large passenger ships collided with each other.

Johan-Ernst Carstens-Johannsen, the officer in charge on the bridge of *Stockholm,* suddenly realized that the unthinkable had occurred. How could a ship that he'd had under constant observation on the port side suddenly behave like that? Why did the unidentified ship cross into the "lane" of *Stockholm?*

During the first few seconds of confusion, all Carstens could do was ask questions without expecting any answers. It is true that other people were on the bridge, but the situation did not lend itself to any protracted conversations.

As a matter of fact, Carstens simply had to trust his own eyes, as well as the numerous reports from the lookouts in the crow's nest and on the wing of the bridge, as to the last crucial maneuver of the oncoming ship. It seemed very strange that the unidentified ship had caught up with *Stockholm* diagonally from behind.

If Carstens had been able to get in touch with Carl-Gustav Quant, the chief steward

of *Stockholm,* right away, his observation would have been confirmed. When Quant looked out of his cabin porthole immediately after the collision, he saw a ship straight ahead of *Stockholm.* He was able to read the name on her stern: *Andrea Doria,* Genoa.

An eyewitness on *Andrea Doria* could also have confirmed Carstens's observations. Fifteen-year-old Martin Sedja, Jr., was standing on deck at the second-class pool. He saw the lights of *Stockholm,* and it seemed to him that she was sheering away to avoid *Andrea Doria.* In an interview he said: "*Stockholm* was approaching us at an angle as if she was trying to avoid a collision with us, but she didn't manage to get out of the way in time."

Carstens knew nothing about those observations as he was walking around on the bridge of *Stockholm,* worried and confused, looking for an explanation of what had actually happened.

Carstens related:

It was only later, through descriptions and eyewitness reports, that we were able to get a rough idea of the reactions of the officers in charge on the bridge of *Andrea Doria.* Our own situation during those first few minutes could be described as "organized disorder."

Captain Nordenson, who had visited the bridge earlier that evening and who had also walked around for a while on the port wing, had returned to his cabin and was to come back before we passed *Nantucket* lightship. We had been instructed to summon him in case of fog or any other unforeseen event.

When Captain Nordenson, whose dayroom was located under the wheelhouse one deck below, heard the rattling of the engine room telegraph, he thought we were entering a foggy area. He was only halfway up the stairs to the bridge when the collision occurred. Those of us who were on the bridge didn't fall over, and neither did Captain Nordenson. Come to think of it, it was strange that the collision was hardly noticed on the passenger decks.

When Captain Nordenson felt the light bump in *Stockholm*'s hull, he thought we'd collided with some kind of wreck underwater or with a fishing boat. There were plenty of those in the area around Nantucket and Cape Cod.

Although as an eyewitness to the collision I understood that the other ship had been seriously damaged, I was naturally most worried about our own ship. How badly damaged was she? Would she be going down? What had happened to the crew who had their cabins in the damaged bow? Had any of the passengers been injured?

There were plenty of questions, but nobody could answer them. We were, however, fully aware that *Stockholm* wouldn't stay afloat for very long if more than one space between the watertight bulkheads was flooded with water. We all thought that there was an immediate risk of that, since *Stockholm*'s bow had quickly sunk about one meter, and she was heeling over 4°.

One of the first things Captain Nordenson wanted to know, of course, was why I hadn't called him earlier. I answered him quite truthfully that there hadn't been any reason whatsoever to do that, since we were sailing in clear weather and visibility was good.

Presently, nearly all the officers came up to the bridge to find out what had happened. Even though I had been in charge on the bridge both before the collision and at the very moment it occurred, nobody reproached me in any way.

Captain Nordenson, who had not seen what had happened, was, like me, in a stressful situation, but he nevertheless made decisions quickly and efficiently. Chief Mate Herbert Källback, Senior Second Mate Lars Eneström, and Junior Second Mate Sven Abenius were instructed to inspect the bow and were soon able to report to the captain about the terrible destruction there. The cabins had been pressed into each other, and there were desperate calls for help from people who had been confined and injured.

It soon became obvious that there had been several casualties and serious injuries aboard *Stockholm*. As luck would have it, many of the crew who had their cabins in the bow were part of the supply service and had escaped because they were working late in the dining rooms, where the evening buffet was just about to be served. All the water pipes in the bow had been broken during the collision, and so had the pipes of the sprinkler system, which triggered the alarm siren in the crew quarters.

After Carstens had put himself at Captain Nordenson's disposal on the bridge to explain, among other things, his opinion of the collision, he made his way to the bow of the ship.

Carstens related:

> In order to get there, we had to walk through a corridor from which a door led to a shaft and a stairwell to the officers' mess. The door was fireproof and had to be forced open. When we'd done that, we found that the entire shaft was filled with water from the broken sprinkler equipment. All this water, around five cubic meters, now came rushing towards us. A hairdresser who was standing in the doorway and I were both washed straight into the nearby hairdressing salon.

Chief Steward Curt Dawe, who was later to assume the main responsibility of organizing the relief work on board, was instructed by Captain Nordenson to check that the passengers were safe and sound. All the cabins were inspected; the passengers were checked against the lists; and everybody was summoned to the lounges. Since there had not yet been any lifeboat practice, it was necessary to demonstrate to everybody how to put on the life vests.

There was never any panic among the passengers. Many of them had been asleep at the time of the collision, and quite a few did not even know for certain what had happened until Captain Nordenson announced on the public address system that *Stockholm* would put out lifeboats to rescue people from *Andrea Doria*. This announcement was made as soon as he realized that *Stockholm* was not in immediate danger of going down.

Stockholm's rescue expedition to *Andrea Doria* had been preceded by an intense and dramatic exchange of telegrams. It all started approximately one hour after the collision with the following message and appeal from Captain Calamai:

> YOU ARE ONE NAUTICAL MILE AWAY FROM US. PLEASE COME IMMEDIATELY AND PICK UP OUR PASSENGERS. THE CAPTAIN.

Captain Nordenson replied:

> SERIOUSLY DAMAGED. THE ENTIRE BOW PRESSED IN AND THE NUMBER ONE HOLD FLOODED. MUST STAY IN OUR PRESENT POSITION. IF YOU CAN PUT OUT YOUR LIFEBOATS, WE CAN PICK YOU UP.

After about fifteen minutes, the following explanation of Captain Calamai's appeal to *Stockholm* to send lifeboats to *Andrea Doria* arrived:

> WE ARE HEELING OVER TOO MUCH. IMPOSSIBLE TO PUT OUR BOATS OVERBOARD. PLEASE SEND LIFEBOATS IMMEDIATELY.

Since it was Captain Nordenson's opinion that *Stockholm* was not in immediate danger, he told Captain Calamai that lifeboats would be sent out within the next forty minutes. At the same time, he ordered mates Källback, Eneström, and Abenius to man the three motor-driven and four of the eight manually operated lifeboats and put them to sea. The remaining four lifeboats were to stay on board *Stockholm*. Captain Nordenson also informed the passengers that the boats that had been put to sea were not intended for them but for the people in distress on *Andrea Doria*.

CHAPTER 9

To *Andrea Doria* in Lifeboats

When *Stockholm*'s lifeboats were launched around 0100 on July 26, it was the beginning of a rescue operation for *Andrea Doria* that was without precedence in the annals of international maritime history. One vessel had never taken care of so many survivors from a sinking ship.

Carstens stated:

In my opinion, this exploit by *Stockholm*'s sailors never received the attention and praise it deserved. Although we have received a number of thank-you notes, all the attention naturally revolved around the sinking of *Andrea Doria* and the allegation that we on *Stockholm* had run into the Italian ship.

Today I sometimes think that it is very important to remember one thing: our lifeboat crews, carrying out a very self-sacrificing duty, sometimes life-threatening out there near the listing *Andrea Doria,* had, by the time it was all over, saved 570 people from the luxury liner and brought them safely over to *Stockholm,* and that included 245 crewmen. Actually, there were two more, but an Italian girl had been taken off by helicopter because she needed immediate medical attention, and one person had died of a heart attack while sitting in a deck chair.

In addition to these 570, there were another 373 people from *Andrea Doria* who

were carried by *Stockholm*'s lifeboats to the other available ships, especially *Ile de France*. Hence, it is an incontrovertible fact that *Stockholm*'s lifeboat crews rescued 943 of the 1,708 people on board *Andrea Doria* in the greatest rescue operation involving civilian ships in world history.

Yet, when Louis S. Rothschild, Undersecretary of the United States Department of Transportation, handed out big plaques commemorating meritorious service to the commanders of *Private William H. Thomas, Ile de France,* and *Cape Ann,* as well as a letter of gratitude to the captain of *Robert E. Hopkins, Stockholm* was not named.

And so it was that despite her mighty rescue efforts, *Stockholm* never appeared in American maritime history under the category of brave ships. A good number of those who manned *Stockholm*'s lifeboats at great risk and saved so many people from *Andrea Doria* no doubt felt that theirs had also been a brave ship.

Stockholm's crew truly responded wholeheartedly, and many of them volunteered to man the lifeboats going to aid those in distress on *Andrea Doria.* A group of stewardesses offered to crew a lifeboat. Captain

At 2300 observed radar echo. At about 1.8 to 1.9 miles distance [saw] two mast-head lights and faint red light. Turned to starboard to show clearly Stockholm's red light. The lookout called out light to port. Ordered starboard, midships and steady so. The turn was about 20 degrees. Went back to the bridge wing and saw Andrea Doria's green light. Then ordered hard starboard, stop and full astern. At the moment of the collision, Andrea Doria sounded. The signal was not received before the collision. The visibility had been good to starboard but closed in rapidly so that Andrea Doria could not be seen [until distance was] 1.8 to 1.9 mile.

Translation of Third Mate Carstens-Johannsen's notes written in a rough deck log after the collision.

Nordenson thanked them for their bravery and willingness to participate, but had to refuse their offer for safety reasons.

One of the passengers, Pastor H. D. Landberg, notified the captain that he had been told by a number of healthy strong men that they were prepared to take out a lifeboat if that was deemed necessary. Again, Captain Nordenson had to politely but firmly decline. In order for the rescue work at *Andrea Doria* to be effective, it required not only enthusiasm and courage, but also and above all good seamanship and knowledge about how to act in the prevailing, very challenging circumstances.

Carstens related:

If everything had been as usual, though nothing was on this terrible night, I would have been replaced on the bridge at midnight. But because of the collision, the whole ship was put on the alert and that meant that every member of the crew had a specific assignment. So I had to remain on the bridge, but I also had the opportunity to inspect the crushed bow. When I asked

Captain Nordenson if I could take out the No. 1 motorized lifeboat, he said that I should first jot down my observations while they were still fresh in my mind.

So I went in behind the wheelhouse, and in a notebook, I wrote down the following, which must be the world's shortest "log-book entry" about the world's thus far biggest (in terms of money) maritime accident involving civilian ships.

At 2300 I observed a radar echo. At a distance of 1.8 to 1.9 nautical miles saw two top lanterns and a weak red light. Turned to starboard to clearly show red light. Lookout rang down and warned about light to port. Ordered starboard, midships, steady as you go. Returned to bridge wing and now saw green lantern. Ordered hard to starboard, stop, and full astern.

At the moment of impact, *Andrea Doria* sounded her horn, but it was not heard prior to the collision. Visibility was good to starboard and port, but a fogbank spread rapidly, which is why *Andrea Doria* had not been spotted until the distance was 1.8 to 1.9 nautical miles.

I haven't seen these notes for thirty years. Confronted now with them in the Gothenburg Maritime Museum, I have to

Three lifeboats filled with survivors left *Andrea Doria* early in the morning as her starboard side sank deeper into the ocean.

admit that I could have expressed myself better, but it's factually accurate enough and ought to have carried considerable weight if it had been presented at a trial. One must make allowances for the wording when considering the circumstances in which it was written.

One could follow the course of events from *Stockholm*'s bridge. Sometimes *Andrea Doria* lay like a brightly lit floating palace; sometimes she disappeared in the fogbanks that were beginning to appear in the area. *Andrea Doria* had experienced palpable difficulties launching her lifeboats. Those on the port side were totally useless; they could not be launched because of her list. At one

point the currents drove the disabled ship right toward *Stockholm,* and there was a risk of a new collision. But *Andrea Doria* drifted past with a margin of about 500 meters.

Carstens explained:

Around quarter to one—about an hour and a half after the collision—three lifeboats from *Andrea Doria* came toward us, almost in a cluster. We saw them quite clearly from *Stockholm*'s bridge, but to help them maneuver, we aimed a spotlight towards the boats. The A deck's opening, which was located on the port side, lay only a couple of meters above water level. There it would be fastest and easiest to help the passengers in the lifeboats aboard. Our people who stood there waiting to help them onto *Stockholm* were amazed to see that the big lifeboats, each with a capacity of 146, were only half full, and most of the occupants were men wearing the gray life jackets of the ship's crew.

Stockholm's crewmen were furious. Such conduct ran in the face of good seamanship, even if these were not sailors in the ordinary sense, but service personnel. Many people on board *Stockholm* would no doubt have preferred to let those first lifeboats that arrived lie beside *Stockholm* and wait or send them back to *Andrea Doria* to exchange their passengers for those who ought to have been rescued first: women and children. One boat was actually pushed away, and its occupants had to bide their time.

Carstens continued:

When things on *Stockholm*'s bridge began to regain some semblance of order, and I had written down my observations, I started to feel a little useless. I judged it was time for my mental well-being to take on a real task, so with Captain Nordenson's approval, I took out the No. 1 lifeboat which was still hanging in its davits far forward on the starboard side. With a sense of relief, I hurried down from the bridge where I had been standing practically nonstop since 2030 the previous evening. Now it was around 0130.

With me in a little boat built for twenty people, I had an engineer and three other crewmen. The weather was very good. Of course, as almost always on the North Atlantic, there were swells, but these were gentle swells that would not disturb the rescue work. I thought about what might have happened if there had been strong winds and heavy seas. The list of casualties on *Andrea Doria* would surely have been considerably larger.

The trip over to *Andrea Doria* took about half an hour. As we approached, we could see the lights of *Ile de France*, which had responded to the call for help. *Cape Ann* and *Thomas* were also nearby. The ocean around us was littered with diverse objects that had fallen out of the big hole on the starboard side close to the bridge after the collision.

What greeted our lifeboats was pretty appalling. Not only the sight of a ship of gigantic proportions about to capsize, but also the terrible sounds that could be heard from afar in clamorous contrast to the stillness of the sea. There were cries and lamentations and prayers, and, from the officers, attempts to use loud commands to impose some kind of order on the prevailing confusion. We also heard the often recurring splashes as people leaped into the water for fear that *Andrea Doria* would suddenly capsize and pull everyone with her down into the deep. A number of people were cast into the ocean in the struggle to escape or simply lost their grip on the ropes out of sheer exhaustion.

I don't believe there is anything more awful than looking at a ship doomed to die just as panicked people are abandoning her. Maybe you can't really fathom the entire tragedy playing out before your eyes at the moment it is happening. The task of saving lives takes over.

But afterwards—for days, years, decades when I am forced to think my way through all of the acts in this drama and make them into a coherent picture—then the powerful feelings return for *Andrea Doria* and for all the people who had relied on her "unsinkability."

But back to lifeboat No. 1. After we got to the Italian luxury liner, we began by cruising along her low starboard side. However, it was obvious that most people on board were on deck farthest back toward the stern, and so we maneuvered there. *Andrea Doria*'s propellers were rotating slowly, and we eventually found ourselves under the sloping deck. Our boat was lifted by the swells and pushed against the hull so that we lost our rudder, but, fortunately enough, nothing worse happened.

What was most astonishing was that no rope ladders had been laid out from the deck, where so many people had gathered, down to the lifeboats. So people made their way down as best they could. Some jumped into the ocean, others came down via fire hoses, cargo nets, indeed anything that could possibly be used to escape the sinking ship.

Nobody who came aboard our boat was badly injured, but several were covered with blood and smeared with oil. I could only guess at how many people from *Andrea Doria* we took into our boat. Maybe twenty-five or thirty, maybe forty. In that situation, you don't count the survivors, you rescue them. We laid low in the water, but it was calm weather, and we had no reason to anticipate any further misfortune.

And so began the arduous journey back to *Stockholm.* Since the rudder was broken, I had to use an oar to steer with. As we left *Andrea Doria,* the heavy currents carried her farther away. The screams and shouts grew fainter as we slowly made our way back to *Stockholm.* Searchlights from both *Andrea Doria* and *Ile de France* lit up the ocean, but beyond the cones of light lay lifeboats that did not dare approach the disabled vessel for fear that she would capsize at any moment.

Lifeboats are not always easy to maneuver. Naturally, it's worse if they are heavily loaded and have a low freeboard. That made it really important to maintain order among the survivors in *Stockholm*'s lifeboat No. 1.

Many people had been panicky when they came aboard the lifeboat but most had quickly calmed down once they had finally been rescued after waiting for hours. Actually, there was only one woman who began to jump about and scream. As we were overloaded, I was worried that general confusion would arise and that we would tip over. I had learned that in a panic situation, you should be very firm if you're going to have a chance to restore order. So I said very

sharply to her to sit still, and she nicely sat back down. But soon she began to carry on again and anxiety began to spread. The same thing happened a third time, and each time I pushed her back down gently but firmly. Finally, she appeared to sit there calmly in her place.

We discovered the reason for her peculiar behavior after we had deposited our passengers on *Stockholm* and hoisted our boat. It turned out that the exhaust pipe that passed under the thwarts had rusted badly and the thwart had simply burned up. Naturally, it must have been very uncomfortable to be sitting just there, and I apologized to her for what had happened during our crossing.

Otherwise, the round trip to *Andrea Doria* had gone well, except that we were missing a boy from among the crew we had taken on board. We found him later. He had been terror stricken and had hidden under the fuel tank.

For myself, I thought it felt good to get off *Stockholm* for a couple of hours and take part in the rescue operation. For some reason, I had left my shoes and cap on *Stockholm*'s deck when I sailed out to *Andrea Doria* in the lifeboat. I can understand Captain Nordenson's being somewhat surprised when I returned to the bridge a couple hours later in a uniform smeared with blood and oil, wearing clean white shoes and a white cap without a spot on it!

CHAPTER 10

Tragedies in the Night— The Rescued and the Dead

The collision off Nantucket had claimed fifty-six lives—fifty-one on *Andrea Doria* and five on *Stockholm*. The fates of these people, and the experiences of those seriously injured and dramatically rescued, were front-page news.

Most of the publicity focused on "the miracle girl," the little fourteen-year-old in yellow pajamas who had been found shocked and injured on *Stockholm*'s mangled foredeck. She was lying in a tangle of twisted steel and timber when Bernablé Polance Garciá from Cadiz, a steward on board *Stockholm*, caught sight of her and began crawling to her rescue.

Garciá had come up on deck a short while earlier. He was suffering from seasickness and had been suddenly knocked off his feet when *Stockholm* collided with the black ship with the white superstructure that loomed up obliquely from the stern. When Garciá struggled to his knees, he could see the other ship heeled over in front of *Stockholm*'s bow and he could read her name—*Andrea Doria*.

To Garciá's amazement, the little girl's first words were in Spanish. "Where's my mommy, who are you?" Garciá replied in Spanish, "We'll find your mommy. Me, I'm from Cadiz."

Garciá labored resolutely with two other *Stockholm* crewmen to free the girl, who lay behind a 75-centimeter-high gunwale 25 meters in on what had once been *Stockholm*'s foredeck. Garciá worked like a man in a trance. His berth had been in *Stockholm*'s bow and many of his fellow crewmen had been lying asleep in the crew's quarters at the time of the collision.

The little girl cried and begged, "I want to go to my mommy." She wailed as she was carried to the sick bay. *Stockholm*'s chief purser, Curt Dawe, was hurrying from his office up to the bridge when he stumbled upon Garciá and the girl.

"What happened to the girl?" asked Dawe. Garciá and the other crewmen assumed she had been in a "forbidden area" on the foredeck, off limits to passengers at the time of the collision. Dawe pulled a passenger list out of one of his pockets and asked, "What's your name?"

"Linda Morgan," answered the girl.

Dawe searched through the list. No Morgan. He looked under "C" for Cianfarra, the girl's mother's last name. No luck.

The girl looked around and uttered the magical words, "I was on the *Andrea Doria*. But where am I now?"

The mystery of the girl on the foredeck was solved! Linda Morgan had been lying in the outer berth in stateroom 52 on the upper deck of *Andrea Doria*. Her eight-year-old half-sister Joan had been in the inner berth. The girls had drawn lots for the attractive outer berth as they came on board.

Linda—traveling with her sister, her mother Jane Cianfarra, and her stepfather Camille Cianfarra, a foreign correspondent for the *New York Times* in Madrid—won the outer berth. The family was on its way home to the United States for vacation.

Eight-year-old Joan, in the inner berth, had died at the instant of the collision, whereas fourteen-year-old Linda was saved because her berth had been lifted over onto *Stockholm*'s foredeck.

By the time this book was written, thirty years after the collision, Linda Morgan had come to terms with her memories. "I was so young when all that happened," she said. "Children do have an ability to forget and move on."

Linda Morgan's stepfather Camille Cianfarra died as a result of the collision, as did her little sister Joan. Her mother Jane Cianfarra had been wedged tightly into stateroom 56, having been hurled there from her own stateroom 54. She had seen her husband die, and she had watched another woman desperately struggling to free herself, only to succumb as rescuers finally arrived.

Jane Cianfarra never recovered emotionally from the catastrophe. She was af-flicted with depression every year on the anniversary of the collision. She died of a stroke eleven years after the collision when she was only fifty-one years of age.

"But at least I had my real father and my mother alive when I grasped the extent of the catastrophe at sea," recalled Linda Morgan. "After all, so many people lost everything." Linda's father, radio broadcaster Edward P. Morgan, had originally been told that his daughter was among the victims— he had talked on the radio about how it feels to lose a beloved child. But just a few hours later, he was relieved to learn that Linda had been found, and he had his daughter back again.

"Daddy kept in touch with 'the man from Cadiz' for many years," said Linda Morgan. "Daddy helped him with a little money when he moved to Canada to open a coffee shop. Later we lost touch. As far as I know, my rescuer died some years ago."

Linda Morgan never used the name Cianfarra after the accident. She married Phillip Hardberger, a lawyer, and had a daughter. "I suppose I am a perfectly ordinary middle-class American," she says with a laugh. "But I make the most of everything in life. My husband flies, and I happily accompany him. We spend a good deal of time outdoors, and we go on a lot of canoe trips. We climb mountains and go camping."

Linda Morgan-Hardberger suffered no permanent physical harm from the collision. The only mementos are the scars from the several operations required to reconstruct her crushed kneecaps. She does not think very often of the violent collision and how she became "the miracle girl." But her daughter is eager to hear about what happened.

"She asks and I answer," her mother stated. "But of course, memories sometimes return with no prompting—that collision did destroy a young family. I imagine that I react a lot more than most other people do when there's news of a major catastrophe," Linda Morgan continued. "Like when the space shuttle *Challenger* exploded. Naturally, a lot of people were shocked and saddened. But I think it hits me even harder. After all, I know exactly what something like that implies for an entire family."

Linda Morgan was indeed "the miracle girl" of the catastrophe. Word of her incredible rescue spread rapidly on *Stockholm* as she lay tucked in bed in the sick bay during the night of July 25 and 26. Beside her was her red autograph book, signed by such people as Jimmy Stewart, Gregory Peck, Cary Grant, and John Steinbeck, whom she had met through her father. That book had been found on *Stockholm*'s foredeck.

When Linda Morgan left *Stockholm,* she had her autograph book with her, along with a little compact she had received as a souvenir from Chief Purser Curt Dawe, who also visited her later in the hospital in New York.

Surprisingly, the atmosphere on *Stockholm* immediately after the collision was comparatively calm. Of course, passengers in the lounge ran to the windows, and many went up on deck. But in the dark, they could see very little of the dramatic rescue—only a dim light came from *Andrea Doria.* The crew prevented the passengers from going onto *Stockholm*'s demolished foredeck, and the damaged area on the lower deck was closed off. Five crewmembers from *Stockholm* had been entered on the list of those dead, missing, or seriously injured. All had been found in the forward crew's quarters. No passengers were on the list.

At the beginning, though, it was suspected that one passenger was among the dead. When Linda Morgan was being carried away from the foredeck, crewman Waldemar Trasbo caught sight of the motionless body of a woman. Could it be the

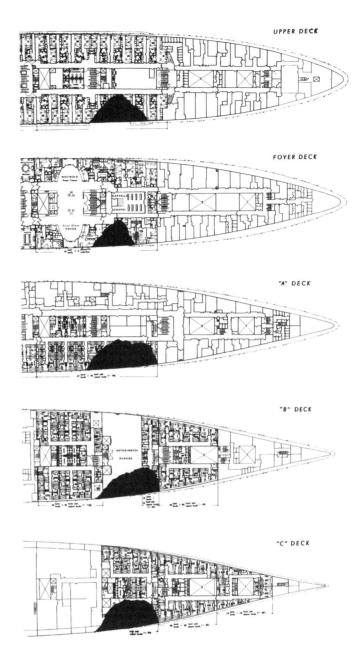

Five passenger decks of *Andrea Doria* were affected by the collision, as shown by the areas indicated in black. Most affected were the passengers—primarily immigrants—in the cabins on C deck. Many passengers escaped harm because, at the time of the collision, they were in one of the ballrooms.

little girl's mother? And why, Trasbo wondered, had the two of them been on the foredeck which was off limits to the ship's passengers?

Trasbo crawled over to the woman. She was sitting straight up, and he took hold of one arm. To his horror, it separated from her body. Shaken, he grasped her long red hair firmly and tried to pull her further in on the foredeck. Trasbo came away with her hair in his hand, and when he crawled back, he watched as the woman fell into the sea.

But the woman was not a passenger on *Stockholm*, nor was she Linda Morgan's mother. Through Trasbo's description, she was identified as Jeanette Carlin, a passenger on *Andrea Doria*. She and her husband had declined the invitation of some friends to continue the evening in their company and retired for the night to their stateroom, which was number 46 on the upper deck.

Jeanette Carlin was in bed reading when her husband Walter, a successful lawyer in Brooklyn, New York, went into the bathroom. A minute later he was knocked to the floor, and when he stumbled back into the stateroom, his wife had disappeared. Her bed and the bed table and lamp were also gone. A huge hole gaped in the ship's hull.

Report of vessel's steward
MS *Stockholm* Voyage 103 eastbound

Vessel departed from New York, Wednesday, July 25, 1956 at 1131.

The crew consisted of 213 persons of which 156 were in the steward's department.

The vessel had 534 passengers, of which 18 were in first class and 516 in tourist class.

Shortly after 2300 on the evening of July 25, the collision with another vessel occurred. First a powerful crash was felt, and three noises immediately followed. A number of passengers were knocked down. It later became known that the other ship was *Andrea Doria*. Our fo'c'sle was seriously damaged. Immediately we undertook rescue work to save those who were injured and find crewmembers who were missing.

Immediately after the collision the crew was checked. Because of the collision Elis Osterberg died and the following were missing: Evert Svensson, Kenneth Jonasson, and Sune Steen. Refer to the log abstract and to the medical report.

The next morning, July 26, the following were taken from the site by helicopter, together with a child rescued from *Andrea Doria* who was 4 years old. She was Norma di Sandro, and she died.
    Vilhelm Gustavsson
    Alf Johansson
    Arne Smedberg
    Lars Falk
    Alf Johansson died after arrival at Nantucket.

On the foredeck, as a result of the collision, a young girl was found—Linda Morgan Cianfarra (fourteen years old) who had been in Cabin 52 on *Andrea Doria*. She had been injured in the left shoulder and in her knees. She was taken care of by the ship's hospital.

Among the passengers a few minor injuries were found. See the ship's doctor's report.

When it was found that the vessel would remain afloat, the master announced this fact over the loudspeaker. No lifeboat alarm was sounded.

Report by *Stockholm*'s steward.

Walter Carlin felt the raw, damp air of the Atlantic; he saw an ocean black as night.

As it turned out, Jeanette Carlin had been lifted over onto *Stockholm* from *Andrea Doria* just as Linda Morgan had been. *Stockholm*'s bow had killed Jeanette while a trip to the bathroom had saved her husband.

Captain Nordenson delivered his first announcement to *Stockholm*'s passengers through the intercom system soon after the collision. By then the damage to *Stockholm* had been assessed, and she had been judged reasonably seaworthy. Captain Nordenson spoke to the passengers from the bridge: "May I have your attention, please. This is the captain speaking. We have collided with the Italian liner *Andrea Doria,* but there is no danger. There is no cause for worry."

The captain sounded calm and collected. *Stockholm*'s slight list was hardly noticeable. Some passengers retired to their cabins; others remained in the lounge. There was never any sign of panic on board.

```
     Lifeboats from Andrea Doria had arrived, and the survivors from
Andrea Doria were taken aboard through both A deck doors. When SS Ile
de France came to the scene of the tragedy about two and a half hours
after the collision, she took over 400 survivors aboard. The total
saved were 245 crew and 327 passengers, a total of 572 persons from
Andrea Doria.
     Some of the survivors were taken to the tourist-class dining room,
some to space on the veranda deck. The sick and the wounded were sent
to the ship's hospital. Among our passengers were found three doctors
who stood by and were of enormous help. Also among the survivors were
two doctors who helped tremendously.
     The survivors were given necessities: bedding, clothing, and
refreshments (coffee, water, cigarettes). Immediately after the
collision all serving of wine and spirits was forbidden.
     Lifeboats from our ship rescued about 370 from Andrea Doria; these
people were brought to other ships, especially Ile de France.
     With two helicopters, five of the seriously injured were brought to
Nantucket, where one man died. The helicopter went on to Boston,
Massachusetts (Brighton Marine Hospital), and arrived at about 0900 in
the morning.
     After arrival at New York, fifteen injured and ill patients were
brought to St. Vincent's and Roosevelt Hospitals in ambulances.
     An Italian girl from Andrea Doria, about four years old, died at
Brighton Marine Hospital, Boston, Massachusetts, two days after arrival
because of serious injury.
     On July 26, 1956, at 1645 one of Andrea Doria's passengers died of
heart failure while lying in a deck chair on Stockholm's sun deck. He
had had chest pains during the rescue from Andrea Doria but did not ask
for help or any medicine from the dispensary.
     Work with the injured did not cease until after arrival in New York
Harbor on July 27, 1956.
     The vessel arrived at New York Pier 97, North River, Friday, July
27, at 1205.
     On Saturday, July 28, at 1922 the vessel was towed to Bethlehem
Steel's Shipyard at Fifty-sixth Street, Brooklyn, New York. The vessel
was drydocked at 0020 on the night of July 29.
```

CHAPTER 11

Andrea Doria Sinks and *Stockholm* Returns to New York

The night of July 25 and 26, 1956, had been a nightmare for Johan-Ernst Carstens–Johannsen and his shipmates on board *Stockholm*. They had all been frantically busy, and hardly anyone got a wink of sleep.

Carstens stated:

Sometimes, when the accident has come up in our conversations, my friends and acquaintances have asked me what it was like to be involved in a major maritime disaster. I've always answered truthfully: when the first shock had subsided, I felt very little, maybe because I didn't have much time to think about how I felt after the initial confusion on the bridge. It may have been the job I had to do that kept me from thinking. One thing that most certainly helped me get over the terrible thing that had happened to me was that I got the chance to set out in the No. 1 lifeboat. It meant that I was given a clearly specified task which was exciting and demanded my full attention. When you're sitting in a small boat and you're in charge of both the crew and the survivors, you concentrate so hard that everything else fades into the background.

As I was standing on the bridge on the morning of July 26 after passengers and crew had been rescued, watching through my binoculars as *Andrea Doria* gradually went down, it all seemed to me like an unpleasant and unreal dream—something I hadn't taken part in. The red glow to the east promised a beautiful summer's day.

As early as 0238 on board *Andrea Doria* Captain Calamai had radioed a telegram to *Stockholm* to be forwarded to the United States Coast Guard. Calamai wrote:

IN POSITION 40°30'N, 69°53'W COLLISION. WE NEED THE ASSISTANCE OF TUGBOATS IMMEDIATELY.

At 0308 the Coast Guard replied:

THE COAST GUARD CUTTER *EVERGREEN* WILL ARRIVE AT THE POSITION INDICATED WITHIN FOUR OR FIVE HOURS.

To Captain Calamai, this was an extremely long wait. He was fully aware that *Andrea Doria* could be salvaged if she were towed toward the island of Nantucket, where she could be placed on the banks with her

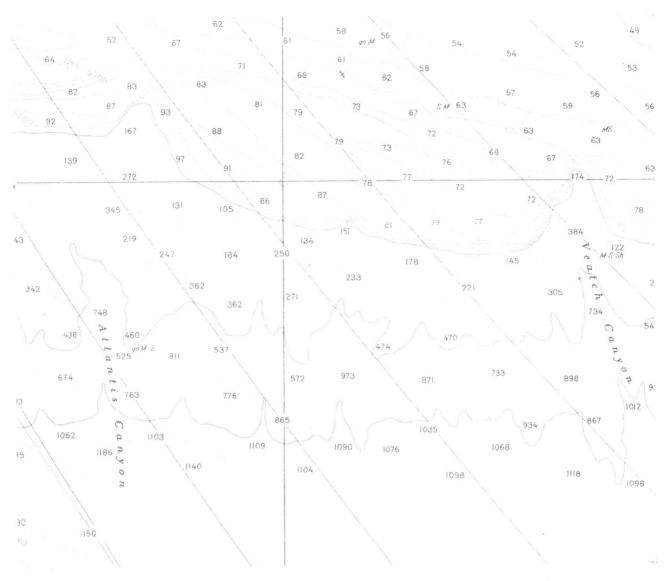

The chart shows the continental shelf and the abrupt increase in depth from less than 100 to almost 2,000 meters (about 50 to 1,100 fathoms).

upper decks above the surface of the water. At a distance of 20 nautical miles, the ocean was only 17 fathoms deep. Immediately after the collision, Captain Calamai had in fact made an attempt to take the ship into more shallow water. When he pushed the speed lever forward slowly, the undamaged turbine to port started up, but the ship shook in such an alarming way that he had to give up the attempt.

It was then that Captain Calamai understood that he would not be able to repeat his feat from World War II, when he took a damaged Italian submarine into shallow water, thus saving both the vessel and the crew.

Soon after the failed attempt to move *Andrea Doria*, the Coast Guard informed the captain that assistance was on the way. Captain Calamai took his second mate Guido Badano by the arm and said in a low voice, "If you are rescued, would you go to Genoa and see my family? Tell them that I did all I could."

Mate Badano, pointing at the lifeboats spread out around *Andrea Doria*, answered, "Captain, we'll all be rescued." Calamai did not answer, and the second mate realized that he was prepared to go down with his ship. A little after 0400, Staff Captain Magagnini, the second-in-command, reported to Captain Calamai that all the passengers had been evacuated. A number of crewmembers remained gathered on the bridge.

The officers on the bridge of *Stockholm* pointed their binoculars at *Andrea Doria,* which had been almost completely abandoned. Suddenly, they spotted a man who seemed to be climbing the hull of the ship. He would later be identified as Robert Lee Hudson, an American sailor who had been injured and was traveling to the United States on board *Andrea Doria* for hospital treatment. The medical staff of *Andrea Doria* had given Hudson sleeping pills and painkillers, and he had slept through the collision. When he woke up, it was pitch dark, and the corridor outside his cabin was quiet and empty. He groped his way up on deck and saw hawsers hanging down the side of the ship. Hudson shouted in the direction of some lifeboats, and a boat from the oil tanker *Robert E. Hopkins* began to steer toward him. As far as is known, Hudson was the last passenger to be rescued from *Andrea Doria* and the only one to be taken aboard *Hopkins.*

This incident led to speculation that the cabins of *Andrea Doria* may not have been carefully checked after the collision, even though Captain Calamai had given strict instructions to that effect. Therefore, there could have been other passengers who did not wake up, if, for example, they had also taken sleeping pills.

The officers on the bridge of *Stockholm* did not notice Hudson being taken on board the lifeboat. They did notice, however, that *Andrea Doria* was heeling over 40° and that it was doubtful she would stay afloat until the towing assistance arrived. Magagnini said, "There's nothing else we can do. We can wait for the tugboats in our lifeboats."

Calamai replied, almost inaudibly, "You go, I'll stay."

Captain Calamai then summoned Monsignor Sebastian Natta, the ship's priest. The two men began to speak in very low voices when Magagnini interrupted them, "It's pointless, Captain, but if you're going to stay, so will we." Some twenty officers now remained on board *Andrea Doria,* and there were some forty crewmen in two lifeboats nearby.

Captain Calamai had made a gesture indicating that he was prepared to leave his ship. According to the other officers, he looked like an old man. His eyes were lifeless, his body was sagging, with his shoulders slouched forward. He was escorted down to lifeboat No. 11 on the boat deck. The men began to get into the lifeboat. After all the remaining men had left *Andrea Doria,* it was the captain's turn. Staff Captain Magagnini looked up at the boat deck where Captain Calamai remained. "Leave," he cried. "I'm staying." Magagnini then left the lifeboat and climbed back on deck. "If you don't come with us, sir, we'll all go back," he said. Magagnini climbed back into the lifeboat and waited. Finally, Captain Calamai nodded down to the other officers.

The captain of *Andrea Doria* climbed down into the last lifeboat very slowly as if he were a very, very old man. It was then 0530. The fog had lifted, and the sun was rising at the horizon, promising a beautiful summer day. *Andrea Doria* was lying on her side like a ghost ship when the last lifeboat reluctantly left her.

Captain Calamai and his crew were still hoping for towing assistance. At 0615 *Ile de France* was preparing to go back to New York. The captain of *Ile de France* informed the captain of *Stockholm* by telegraph that his ship would turn around "at full speed." The damaged *Stockholm* remained still, her anchor chains firmly wedged to the bottom.

Andrea Doria continued to list to starboard, making it impossible to launch the lifeboats. Photo from the collection of William P. Quinn.

Ile de France made a wide circle around the abandoned *Andrea Doria*. The flag was hoisted and lowered three times while the steam whistle sounded three long signals. Many of the crew in *Andrea Doria*'s lifeboats, positioned only a few hundred meters from the doomed ship, cried openly.

Soon afterward, a small aircraft buzzed overhead, carrying reporters and photographers and circling around *Andrea Doria* for the best possible pictures. Many of the crew could not help but compare them to vultures circling over a dying animal.

At 0740 the helicopters finally arrived. *Stockholm* had asked for them in one insistent telegram after another. They were not able to land on the deck of *Stockholm* to take care of the most seriously injured, so stretchers were lowered. Five injured people were flown to hospitals in Nantucket and Boston. Two of them died: a little girl who had been thrown into a lifeboat by her father and one crewman who had been in the bow of the ship.

Ever since the collision, *Stockholm* had been held in place by her anchor chains. The full length of the chains had been released, but the ends were still attached in the chain locker. After about one hour's strenuous work by First Mate Herbert Källback, Senior Second Mate Lars Eneström, and First Boatswain Ivar Eliasson, these

Andrea Doria listing seriously to starboard. Courtesy Francis J. Duffy.

chains were successfully cut off. Parts of *Stockholm*'s bow and also her anchor chains rumbled into the ocean as the ship was maneuvered back and forth. It was a heroic effort these men made on board *Stockholm*, especially considering the fact that they had also been struggling all night long to rescue survivors from *Andrea Doria*.

When *Stockholm* lost this section of its bow, it lost the "material" documentation to prove that *Andrea Doria* had rammed *Stockholm*. Fortunately, photographs taken previously survived.

Besides *Stockholm*, several other ships were around *Andrea Doria* at the time: the tanker *Hopkins*, the American transport vessels *Thomas* and *Johan E. Kelley, Manaqui* from Honduras, the British freighter *Tarantia*, and the Norwegian *Free State. Ile de France* and *Cape Ann* were heading for New York.

The Coast Guard cutter *Evergreen* had arrived at 0806. At 0830 the American de-

stroyer *Allen* arrived and came up alongside the lifeboat in which Captain Calamai was seated, but he refused to leave it. The cutter *Hornbeam*, which was equipped with tow hooks, was sighted at 0855. Calamai went on board the cutter to wait for the reply to the following radio message sent by *Evergreen* at 0902 to the Coast Guard in Boston:

THE *HORNBEAM* IS STANDING BY *ANDREA DORIA*. TAKING ON BOARD 45 CREWMEN FROM LIFEBOATS, AMONG OTHERS, THE CAPTAIN. LOOKING INTO THE POSSIBILITY OF TOWING THE STEAMSHIP.

There was an immediate reply:

THE *HORNBEAM* SHOULD NOT TRY TO TOW. ITALIAN LINE WILL CONTACT MERRITT CHAPMAN AND SCOTT AS WELL AS MORAN TOWING. ASSISTANCE BY EITHER OR BOTH EXPECTED.

In the last stages of sinking, *Andrea Doria* lies on her starboard side, her funnel touching the water. An empty lifeboat drifts away at right. United States Coast Guard photo, from the collection of William P. Quinn.

The Captain was informed of this reply. He did not say anything. But when he gazed out over the ocean glittering in the sun, he knew what Italian Line probably did not: it was only a matter of half an hour, or perhaps an hour, before *Andrea Doria* would go down.

The final stage of the death struggle of *Andrea Doria* began at 0945. Technically speaking, she capsized; she was flooded with water from stem to stern. At 1002 the funnel showing the Italian colors of white, red, and green sank under the surface of the water. The last section to be seen was the stern with the name *Andrea Doria,* Genoa. At 1009 she disappeared from view completely. The ocean was boiling with bubbles, and various objects from inside *Andrea Doria* and from

her decks were floating around. The Italian luxury liner had come to rest.

Evergreen radioed to the Coast Guard:

SS *ANDREA DORIA* WENT DOWN AT A DEPTH OF 225 FEET AT 40°29'N, 69°50'W.

Some of *Andrea Doria*'s crew followed the drama from the decks of *Stockholm, Allen,* and *Hornbeam.* Many of them emptied their pockets of anything that might remind them of *Andrea Doria.* They did not want anything to remind them of the sunken ship.

Carstens and the other officers were standing on the captain's bridge of *Stockholm,* witnessing the various stages of the wreck. Sten Johansson was back in the crow's nest. "As she was going down, her black hull looked like a diving whale," Carstens says. "We stood there without moving, our flag was lowered, and then *Stockholm* very slowly began her return voyage to New York."

There was naturally considerable anxiety about what might happen to *Stockholm* while approaching New York. Would the watertight bulkhead which now formed the new stem be able to withstand the strain once the ship was sailing again? It is true that the ship was escorted by the Coast Guard cutter *Tamaroa* and by the cutter *Owasco*, but those were both small ships with limited capacity to take care of all the people on board if anything serious were to occur. *Stockholm* had assumed responsibility for the lives of many people. In all there were 1,319 people on board but room for only 846 in the lifeboats.

Captain Nordenson had telegraphed *Ile de France* asking the French ship to escort *Stockholm* to New York. To his great surprise, *Ile de France* refused to do so, referring to the fact that she was already delayed and needed to get back on schedule. *Ile de France* did not seem to take into account that *Stockholm* was a badly damaged ship with too many people on board.

Carstens related:

I'm sure we would have felt safer if *Ile de France* had escorted us to New York. Of course, one can understand that the French shipping company wanted to keep to its sailing schedule, but I've a distinct feeling that the ovation *Ile de France* was given when she sailed into New York with all the survivors from *Andrea Doria* on board would have been considerably more quiet if *Stockholm* had met with disaster while returning to New York.

Stockholm was lucky to have stayed afloat. The watertight bulkhead stood like a sail in a stiff wind. It looked very unpleasant, even scary. And if it were to break, *Stockholm* would also go down fairly quickly.

Who would then assist all those people *Stockholm*'s lifeboats couldn't hold?

Now that we had begun our voyage back to New York and got back into a certain routine, I thought I could return to my cabin and get some sleep. Imagine my surprise when I entered it and found that it had been emptied. There had been burglars, and all the drawers had been pulled out. There were many others who had the same experience. No one knows who the thieves were. We didn't usually lock our cabins while we crossed the Atlantic. People at sea trust each other. There is some kind of code of honor, and things very rarely disappear.

Since nobody reported the thefts, nothing appeared in the purser's report. It would have been pointless to start an investigation in the confusion on board *Stockholm*. People were lying all over the place—in corridors, lounges, and on deck. It was hardly a good time to bring up something like stealing at that moment.

The voyage back to New York was more or less uneventful and, as a matter of fact, quicker than estimated. Our average speed of 8.4 knots was surprising, considering that *Stockholm* had no bow. Taking over the watch on the bridge was done according to the usual schedule, which was also somewhat surprising.

In the evening on July 26, Carstens did not know if he was to have the watch between 2030 and 2400, that is, the same time period during which *Stockholm* had collided with *Andrea Doria*. He thought that both Captain Nordenson and Chief Mate Källback would be on the bridge, especially since it was getting dark, and they were still in the precarious situation of sailing a seriously damaged ship. It also crossed his mind that the captain might not find it appropriate for Carstens to have the watch during that particular period.

Those were the main reasons why he waited for a quarter of an hour before going up to the bridge. The mate who had the watch called to ask why he hadn't shown up.

Stockholm's bow after the collision, before a large section of the port side, together with the anchor chains, fell into the ocean. As can be seen, the bow was "cut" diagonally indicating that *Stockholm* and *Andrea Doria* collided with each other at an angle of about 30 to 45°.

Carstens related:

I felt quite nervous about being on the bridge again and being the only one in charge. But at the same time, I saw it as a feather in my cap that Captain Nordenson still had confidence in me. After Senior Second Mate Eneström had been relieved and returned to his cabin, Captain Nordenson, who had been on duty for more than twenty-four hours, called and told me that he was rather tired and was going to bed.

He instructed me to call the chief mate if we ran into fog and to call him if anything out of the ordinary happened. Of course, nothing unusual happened, but even situations that could be classified as normal at sea can entail certain elements of real excitement. After all, *Stockholm* was sailing in one of the world's most heavily trafficked fairways.

When *Stockholm* finally docked at Pier 97 on Fifty-seventh Street, which was the usual berthing place of Swedish America Line, the scene was totally different from the one that normally takes place at the arrival of a passenger ship. A chain of

Full view of *Stockholm* shows the extent of damage to the bow. From the collection of William P. Quinn.

police officers shut out the crowds of people who had come down to the Hudson River to look at the seriously damaged ship.

Interest had been reaching a peak during the previous few hours, since there had been both radio and television broadcasts about the incident for a long time. Eleven ambulances were waiting outside the area that had been cordoned off, and the Red Cross was there with stretchers, doctors, and nurses. There were also "wardrobes on wheels"—these held various kinds of garments. Coffee was served. The Traveler's Aid Society as well as other relief and charity organizations had sent representatives to meet the ship.

The media crowd from the press, radio, and television was enormous. Hundreds of reporters and photographers tried to get on board, mainly to get an interview with Captain Nordenson, but Carstens was also in great demand.

The first ones to be allowed to go on shore were the survivors from *Andrea Doria*. They were 570 in all, 245 of whom were crew. The most sensational story was no doubt that of movie star Ruth Roman, who was reunited with her three-year-old son Richard, called Dickie. She had been rescued from *Andrea Doria* by *Ile de France*, which had returned to New York in triumph the previous evening. Then came

```
=
HEMLAND GOETBG
AMERLINE GOETBG
GÖTEBORG DEN 26/7 1615


VI HAR ERHÅLLIT FÖLJANDE TELEGRAM FRÅN HAEMLAND NEW YORK:


2210/119 NEWYORK 41 W 26/7 0125 VIA SVERIGERADIO FÖRDRÖJT TILL
FÖLJD AV FELAKTIG ADRESS=


SORRY INFORM ANDREADORIA AND STOCKHOLM COLLIDED WEDNESDAY ABOUT
2330 OFF NANTUCKITLIGHTSHIP STOP NO DIRECT WORD FROM STOCKHOLM
ABOUT HER CONDITION AND UNABLE CONTACT HER BUT RADIO REPORTS
NUMBER ONE HOLD FLOODED STOP WILL REVERT WHEN HAVE FURTHER
INFORMATION
                    LUNDBECK+


HEMLAND GOETBG
AMERLINE GOETBG
```

The official announcement of the collision between *Stockholm* and *Andrea Doria* was delayed because the telegram was erroneously sent to "Amerline," the telegram address of the freight department, instead of to "Hemland," the telegram address of the passenger department of Swedish America Line's home office.

the passengers of *Stockholm,* only a few of whom had suffered injuries, all minor.

Naturally, those who had been involved in the collision realized they would be exposed to a veritable ordeal by the press. Accompanied by representatives of Italian Line, *Andrea Doria*'s Captain Calamai, who had been taken into New York the previous evening on board the American destroyer *Allen,* read a well-prepared statement which said the company blamed *Stockholm* for what had happened.

Swedish America Line, however, decided to keep a low profile on the question of guilt. Charles Haight, one of the foremost American experts on maritime law, had been contacted immediately after the accident. He and his colleagues met *Stockholm*'s crew at the quarantine station, so they could prepare for the press attack while sailing into the harbor.

Carstens related:

On my way up to the captain's cabin, I happened to walk behind four gentlemen, one of whom I thought I recognized from his manner of walking. He turned out to be my old friend and classmate from Lund, Jan Ekman, who was in New York interviewing at Haight's law office. It was a very good feeling meeting someone I knew from Sweden.

TELEGRAM

R246 LIVERPOOL 22 27 1329

MR E WIJK HEMLAND GBG

PLEASE ACCEPT OUR SINCERE SYMPATHY IN TRAGIC
INCIDENT IN WHICH YOUR STOCKHOLM INVOLVED
STOP REGARDS

DAWSON CUNARD

TELEGRAM

RT58 LONDON 19 271143

ELT = WIJK HEMLAND GBG

CANADIAN PACIFIC SEND SINCERE SYMPATHY
TERRIBLE ACCIDENT STOCKHOLM WILL GLADLY HELP
ANY WAY POSSIBLE = ARKLE

TELEGRAM

HEMLAND GOETBG
AGENMARIN AN
HEMLAND GOETBG
AGENMARIN AN
HEMLAND GOETBG
AGENMARIN AN   27.7.56   12.45

THE AGENCE MARITIME INTERNATIONALE AND THE COMPAGNIE
MARITIME BELGE CONVEY TO THE SWEDISH AMERICAN LINE THEIR
FEELINGS OF DEEPEST SYMPATHY IN CONNECTION WITH THE
COLLISION OF THE "STOCKHOLM"
ZZZZ
HEMLAND GOETBG
AGENMARIN ANA
HEMLAND GOETBG

TELEGRAM

HEMLAND GOETBG

2250/8 BREMEN 34/33 27/7 1704

HEMLAND GOETEBORG

TO THE TRAGIC COLLISION OF YOUR GOOD SHIP
STOCKHOLM WE SHOULD LIKE TO EXPRESS TO YOU
OUR DEEPFELT SYMPATHY PLEASE BE ASSURED THAT
OUR THOUGHTS ARE WITH YOU

KORDDEUTSCHER LLOYD BREMEN

Swedish America Line in Gothenburg received many messages of condolence from passenger lines around the world.

```
TELEGR 16 GBG
HEMLAND GOETBG

2250/125 GOTEBORG DEN 28 JUL 1 1956 KL. 13.00 34 W

LUNDBECK
HEMLAND
NEW YORK

CONFER WITH YOUR ITALIAN COLLEAGUE TRY AGREE WITH HIM INSTRUCT COMMANDERS
OFFICERS CREW NOT START BLAMING EACH OTHERS AND AVOID STATEMENTS WHICH ARE
ALL ONLY DEROGATORY TO PASSENGER SHIPPING
    HEMLAND

COLL 2250/125
```

A few days after the collision and the press conference during which Captain Calamai blamed *Stockholm* for the accident, Erik Wijk, president of Swedish America Line, instructed G. Hilmer Lundbeck, Jr., manager of the American organization, to contact the manager of Italian Line in New York in order to try to tone down the verbiage.

During the entire future preparatory hearing, he was a great support to me in an awkward situation. Jan Ekman later became the managing director of Svenska Handelsbanken.

When all the formalities of arrival in New York were over, Swedish America Line arranged a press conference with Captain Nordenson and Charles Haight. Naturally, the press wanted the captain to announce whom he considered to be responsible for the accident, but Nordenson skillfully parried the question by saying that at the present moment he didn't want to put the blame on anybody. He emphasized, however, that he didn't fear the future hearing and was waiting for it to begin with great interest.

That reply, which was so totally different from the uncompromising statement made by Captain Calamai, aroused great sympathy among the press and the general public.

Those aboard *Stockholm* were finally able to relax a little on the afternoon of July 27. *Stockholm* was back where she had started, safely docked in the harbor. The seriously wounded ship that had refused to die was passed by an endless caravan of cars driving slowly on the highway's west side.

The sun set and it was evening. Another typically hot and humid day in New York was over. The next day, three mighty tugboats were to move *Stockholm* to the big Bethlehem Steel dock, where she was to have a new stem constructed at the price of $1 million.

UNITED STATES DEPARTMENT OF JUSTICE
IMMIGRATION AND NATURALIZATION SERVICE
70 COLUMBUS AVENUE
NEW YORK 23, N.Y.

PLEASE REFER TO THIS FILE NUMBER

DD

July 30, 1956

Swedish American Line
636 Fifth Avenue
New York, New York

Attention:
Mr. Hjalmar Lundbeck,
Resident Manager

Dear Sir,

It is with great pleasure I take this occasion to commend the personnel of your SS "STOCKHOLM", as well as your Landing Agent, Mr. Sepp, for the assistance which they rendered this Service in clearing the SS "ANDREA DORIA" survivors who arrived at this port on July 27, 1956.

I feel particular mention should be made of your Chief Purser, Curt Dawe, who virtually anticipated every need of this Service and was able to furnish our boarding party with complete alphabetical list of all survivors, separated as to crew members and passengers. In addition, Chief Purser Dawe set up an emergency inspection area for our officers and controlled the processing of some 550 survivors.

Again may I say that Mr. Dawe and his staff are worthy of the highest recommendation that I can give them.

Sincerely,

EDW. J. SHAUGHNESSY
District Director
New York District

The officers and crew of *Stockholm* were highly commended for their work both in rescuing and caring for survivors from *Andrea Doria*. The Swedish America Line received letters of appreciation, one from the Italians via the Swedish Embassy, and one directly from the U.S. State Department, in which Chief Purser Curt Dawe and Mr. Sepp, the landing agent of the Swedish America Line, were mentioned.

Washington, 27 July 1956

Dear Sir,

It is my pleasant duty to inform you and the Swedish
America Line that the Italian chargé d'affaires,
Minister Ortona, has telephoned from New York to
express his own as well as the Italian Line's
appreciation of and gratitude for everything done by
the Captain and the crew of the Stockholm in order to
assist and take care of the shipwrecked people from the
Andrea Doria after the collision. Minister Ortona
emphasized that all the passengers, officers and crew
from the Andrea Doria taken care of by the Stockholm
have unanimously commended the first-class seamanship,
the excellent organization and the truly unselfish
helpfulness displayed by the Stockholm's Captain
Nordenson and his crew in these difficult and critical
circumstances. In the midst of their grief for the
casualties and the loss of their ship, the Italians
feel deeply grateful for all this.

I have notified the Foreign Office of the above.

Very truly yours,

Managing Director Lundbeck   Carl Douglas
Swedish America Line   Minister Plenipotentiary
New York   Chargé d'Affaires ad interim

CHAPTER 12

Cape Cod and Nantucket—
A Nautical Graveyard

The collision between *Stockholm* and *Andrea Doria* had occurred off Cape Cod and the islands of Nantucket and Martha's Vineyard. Cape Cod is a peninsula that reaches out like a claw into the Atlantic south of Boston. Nantucket and Martha's Vineyard can be distinguished from the mainland in fair weather. At one time, fishing and whaling were the main sources of income in this area. Today "the cape" and "the islands," as the local inhabitants refer to them, are best known as summer vacation paradises for the affluent residents of New York and Boston, who hobnob with literary, artistic, and political celebrities. Among these the Kennedy clan occupies a unique position.

When one talks with older people on Cape Cod, they often point toward Nantucket and say the fog is "manufactured" there and it is Nantucket that "sends the fog in to us." Nantucket's own residents call her "the little gray lady of the sea."

Everyone who sojourns on Cape Cod and the islands knows precisely what is meant when Nantucket is accused of manufacturing fog. A summer's day can begin with the

most beautiful, clear "beach" weather with miles of visibility, only to be suddenly transformed into a humid foggy afternoon. Many sailors have been caught off guard by the sudden transition from dead calm to stiff wind and heavy seas.

It is only the uninformed who challenge the weather gods in these waters—seafarers and residents have always had respect for the ocean, the reefs, the sandbanks, and the fog.

A visit to the small coastal villages on Cape Cod and the islands can easily be experienced as a passage among shipwrecks. Large and small vessels have been stranded everywhere. The history of ships and crews is preserved in unpretentious museums, in lighthouses, and on monuments in the open air. Many families have photographs hidden in a bureau drawer or perhaps framed on a wall, portraying lost ships. In earlier times, it was a popular pastime to take a walk out through the dunes and inspect the "victims" of storms and fog.

When *Andrea Doria* went down off Nantucket, she was the largest and most luxurious ship ever to have sunk in these waters. Yet, she was only one of at least a thousand vessels that had come to rest in this enormous graveyard of the sea. When the Pilgrims drifted ashore at the foot of Cape Cod in November 1620, they certainly could not have imagined how lucky they were to have been spared from the worst vagaries of the weather there. Despite all their hardships on board the little 180-ton *Mayflower,* the Pilgrims had experienced a relatively untroubled crossing.

The oldest wreck preserved on Cape Cod is a ship that foundered in 1626. It can be seen in Pilgrim Hall in Plymouth where it is displayed beside a memorial to the first Pilgrims and to *Mayflower. Sparrow Hawk,* carrying some Pilgrims from England, took on water and sank on the sandbanks. Her passengers were helped by the little colony of Pilgrims who had arrived in 1620. Some time later, the newly repaired ship set off, this time for Virginia, but was once again driven onto the treacherous sandbanks. There she lay buried until she was uncovered over two hundred years later in 1863 by a mighty storm.

The first lifesaving stations appeared on Cape Cod as early as 1786. It was the little organization known as the Massachusetts Humane Society that built cabins along the beaches containing the barest necessities for stranded crews. Less than a century later, in 1871, the federal government assumed responsibility for sea rescue services. At that time, at least one ship was being lost every fortnight at the cape and the islands.

The fact that Congress allocated funds for sea rescue services along the coasts of America did not mean the end of private initiative. Well into the twentieth century, the salvaging of wrecked ships was a very lucrative occupation. But "the wreckers," as these salvage operations were called, never went after the wreck until they had saved the crew—that was an unwritten law on the cape and the islands.

When the Cape Cod Canal was dug, it separated the peninsula from the mainland, fulfilling a long-standing demand from the shipping industry. The canal was inaugurated in 1914, but it had been discussed seriously since 1776, when George Washington requested an investigation of the prerequisites for such a project.

A number of prospecting efforts were initiated during the nineteenth century. Work was finally begun in 1909, and the canal was inaugurated in 1914. Now seafarers could avoid traveling around Cape Cod and the islands to get into Boston Harbor. They had obtained a safer waterway, and the canal, together with new technological aids, reduced the number of wrecks and close calls.

When *Andrea Doria* sank near *Nantucket* lightship, the drama could not be observed from land. Yet, even today, people promenade along the beaches of Nantucket and gaze out to the area where she lies—the spot is marked on Nantucket's tourist maps. In Nantucket's harbor, one can see the old red *Nantucket* lightship that has been replaced by an electronic buoy.

Serving aboard the lightship was risky. Ships arriving in America from Europe plotted their courses at the lightship, and sometimes they changed course only when it had been sighted. *Titanic's* sister ship *Olympic,* built in 1911, was feared by the crew of *Nantucket* lightship: "One of these days, she'll sink us," complained one crewman to his superiors when *Olympic,* true to character, passed so close to the lightship that her waves nearly submerged *Nantucket.* Just as that crewman had anticipated, the day came when his fears were realized. In May 1934, *Olympic* rammed *Nantucket* in heavy fog and cut her in half. Seven crewmen on the lightship were killed; four were rescued by *Olympic's* lifeboats.

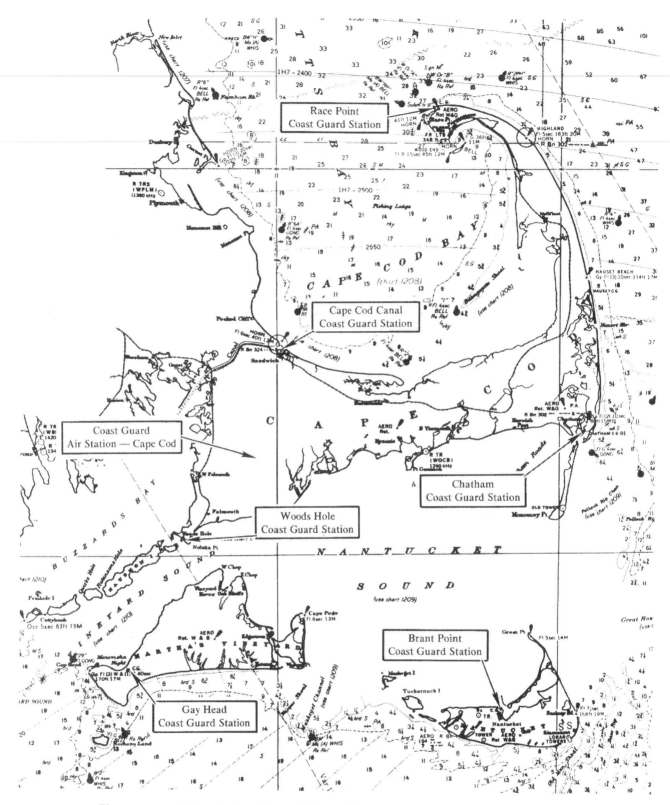

The area around Cape Cod and Martha's Vineyard is a great cemetery for ships. Through the centuries, thousands of ships stranded or sank before lifesaving stations were built. When *Andrea Doria*'s alarm went out, the cutter *Hornbeam* together with others set off from the Woods Hole coastal lifesaving station to rescue Captain Calamai and those aboard his ship.

In 1972, sixteen years after the lifeboat *Hornbeam* had taken the last survivors from *Andrea Doria* on board, she was herself rammed in almost the same location where *Andrea Doria* and *Stockholm* had collided. *Hornbeam* was on her way out to assist *Nantucket* lightship after the Brazilian freighter *Docelago* had struck her just above the waterline. *Hornbeam* was able to make her way back to harbor escorted by two smaller ships.

Perhaps the most complete archive of ship disasters on Cape Cod is that of photographer William P. Quinn. He summarized years of tragedies at sea around Cape Cod, Nantucket, and Martha's Vineyard as follows:

> We will witness more shipwrecks and more storms and more fog. Sailing ships are no longer with us, but they are not forgotten. The remaining bits of wood from once-proud ships serve as anonymous tombstones on our beaches. The roll call of lost ships is long and tragic, and some of their names are and will remain legendary.

An orange buoy today marks the burial place for the greatest legend of them all. Intrepid divers will come to visit her. But salvaged? Probably not. *Andrea Doria* will rest in peace.

CHAPTER 13

Grief and Anger in Italy— Accusations against Sweden

The collision between *Andrea Doria* and *Stockholm* became known in Italy on the early morning of July 26. The newspapers in Genoa published special editions, and stunned and silent crowds filled the Piazza de Ferrari, where the headquarters of Italian Line were located in a large white building. People waited faithfully all day, but the news that came trickling out was very sparse. Nobody could believe that *Andrea Doria* would go down—according to all the information available, she was unsinkable. But as more and more alarming reports arrived, people began to realize how serious the situation was.

Captain Calamai's wife found out about the accident from the headlines on a newspaper kiosk. The following day, she told a news agency about the five hours of torment she endured following the drama minute by minute through frequent radio transmissions and telephone conversations with the offices of Italian Line.

When it was all over and *Andrea Doria* had come to rest at a depth of 70 meters, Signora Calamai, as well as the entire sea-

faring Italian nation, had received a shock that would take a long time to get over.

At the time of the collision, Johan-Ernst Carstens-Johannsen's wife Liliane lived in Lund, Sweden. She said: "I first heard about the accident when I turned on the radio at about ten o'clock on the 26th of July (the collision occurred at 4:10 A.M. local Swedish time). I was shocked, of course, and I called Johan's parents at once. Later that day, I had a telegram from my husband that read as follows: 'All is well. Johan.' After that, the passenger department of Swedish America Line in Gothenburg kept me informed about developments on board *Stockholm*."

As the information officer for Swedish America Line in Gothenburg, Algot Mattsson, the author of this book, received the first message early in the morning. It was the Associated Press in New York who asked over a crackling telephone line if he wanted to comment on the accident. He immediately got in touch with the president of Swedish America Line, Erik Wijk, who thought he'd had an unpleasant dream that he should forget as soon as possible. Unfortunately, a large number of phone calls from the Swedish as well as the foreign media indicated that *Andrea Doria* was in danger of going down and that his "dream" was real.

One of the worst maritime disasters in world history was under way. The official confirmation of the collision was delayed in reaching Swedish America Line because the telegram from the New York office had been sent to the freight department instead of the passenger department. Consequently, the Gothenburg staff had to rely on information from the media during the first few hours.

To the Italians, the sinking of *Andrea Doria* was devastating. Captain Calamai had put the blame for the wreck of *Andrea Doria* on *Stockholm*, and the Italian press accepted this version of the event without any reservation whatsoever.

But as new information about the behavior of *Andrea Doria*'s crew arrived from the scene of the accident, the general public in Italy had another blow—a worse one, perhaps, than the accident itself.

In both the American and Swedish press, many passengers were quoted accusing the crew of *Andrea Doria* of "cowardice, selfishness, fear, and panic," which contributed to the dark shadow that was being cast over the Italian Line as well as over shipping interests in general.

The first lifeboats had returned to *Stockholm* carrying mainly members of *Andrea Doria*'s crew. The eighty-seven survivors who had been taken on board *Cape Ann* had written a letter to the press criticizing the officers and crew of *Andrea Doria* for not providing sufficient instructions and assistance when the ship went down.

These accusations were extremely serious considering that the preliminary hearing was about to begin in New York. When all this information was published, the Italian media flew into a rage.

In Italy, people found it hard to distinguish between purely objective news articles and editorial comments. Like Captain Nordenson, many other Swedish parties involved tried to avoid entering into a controversy with the Italian press and the captain of *Andrea Doria*. But the campaign continued. On August 7, 1956, Erik Wijk wrote the following letter to all Swedish newspapers:

Swedish America Line appreciates the understanding shown by the press for our desire not to enter into issues of responsibility until the underwriters and the lawyers of Swedish America Line have had time to form a clear opinion of the circumstances of the tragic collision between *Andrea Doria* and *Stockholm*.

Today Swedish America Line handed to the United States District Court in New York a petition for a limitation of liability containing important information about the course of events and thereby clarifying certain issues which have hitherto only been insufficiently addressed. It is utterly regrettable that two well-known shipping companies of long standing, both enjoying good reputations in transatlantic traffic, should have to engage in court proceedings. Since, however, so many different interests are at stake and so many complicated problems have come up, it can hardly be avoided that the issue be taken into court and it would be careless of us not to clarify our position in that regard.

We would like to emphasize that the company fully supports the captain, the other officers, and the crew of *Stockholm;* that we have full confidence in them; and that we firmly believe that, once all the facts have been presented and analyzed, the general public will be as totally convinced as we are that *Stockholm* was not at fault.

The Swedish Embassy in Rome kept the Foreign Office posted continuously on the reactions of the Italians to the collision. One such piece of information was a letter from the embassy to "His Excellency the Foreign Secretary" on August 11, 1956, in which an article in *L'Espresso,* a weekly magazine published in Rome, was quoted. It contained a large number of serious allegations against Sweden and against Swedes for their alleged hostility to Italians living in or visiting Sweden.

Relations between Sweden and Italy were complicated by the fact that on September 14, 1954, Swedish America Line had ordered a new passenger liner from the Ansaldo Shipyard in Genoa, the yard that had built *Andrea Doria.* The launching had taken place on April 8, 1956—not quite four months before the collision between *Stockholm* and *Andrea Doria.* The Ansaldo Shipyard and Italian Line were both owned by the Italian state, which had subsidized Swedish America Line by eight million Swedish krona in order for them to place their order there.

The Italian press and general public found it somewhat distressing to learn that Italian taxpayers had been subsidizing a foreign shipping company—particularly one whose ship had, as they saw it, sunk their great pride, *Andrea Doria.*

On the other hand, on ordering *Gripsholm,* as the new ship was to be called, Swedish America Line had praised the Ansaldo Shipyard as being "well known and enjoying an excellent reputation for building many large passenger liners." In this context, Swedish America Line referred to *Andrea Doria* and *Cristoforo Colombo,* two ships built after the war, and to the fact that the shipyard had also previously built the well-known *Rex,* awarded the Blue Ribbon of the Atlantic in 1933.

All these qualifications listed by the owners of *Stockholm* would certainly be very useful if the shipbuilding competence of the yard were questioned at a subsequent trial.

There were no confrontations between the staff of the Ansaldo Shipyard and the Swedish Inspectorate. However, it would have been considered "inappropriate" if *Stockholm*'s Captain Nordenson and Third Mate Carstens-Johannsen were to go to the Italian yard to take the new ship to Sweden. *Gripsholm* arrived in Gothenburg on April 22, 1957.

CHAPTER 14

Stockholm Is Repaired

Immediately after the collision, one of the first questions raised by people in the travel industry—especially in the United States, Sweden, and Italy—was, "What effect will this have on transatlantic passenger traffic?" Air travel had already become a very serious competitor, and many anticipated that all the negative publicity regarding sea voyages which had been generated by the sinking of *Andrea Doria* would produce negative results. In the short run, it did not appear these predictions would come true. As early as August 8, 1956, Swedish America Line's New York office was able to produce statistics on the reactions of the 534 passengers aboard *Stockholm* who were eyewitnesses to most of the drama.

It appeared that at that time passengers had not lost interest in ocean voyages. Seventy percent of *Stockholm*'s passengers rebooked their interrupted trips by ship, many with Norwegian America Line; 22 percent chose to travel by air, and 4 percent decided to defer their plans to the following year. Only 4 percent of *Stockholm*'s passengers canceled their intended voyage to Scandinavia. A number of *Stockholm*'s passengers (148) sailed aboard *Kungsholm*, which left New York for Scandinavia on August 3 with a total of 868 passengers on board. Thanks to the hospitality of the crew, about 100 of these passengers were accommodated in the crew's quarters.

Stockholm had to be repaired as quickly as possible. Otherwise, Swedish America Line would be faced with severe losses from the cancelation of scheduled transatlantic crossings, two five-day cruises to Bermuda, and a thirteen-day cruise to the West Indies planned to depart on November 17. Those cruises would almost conclude the 1956 program for *Stockholm*, with only the Christmas voyage starting from New York on December 8 remaining.

However, meeting the schedule was not meant to be. In the first place, the three transatlantic voyages and one Bermuda cruise would have to be canceled unless *Stockholm* could obtain a new bow with "express speed." Inasmuch as the vessel could not make extensive voyages (and certainly not a transatlantic voyage) without a new bow, there was nothing else to do but choose a nearby yard that could do the job. Bethlehem Steel in Brooklyn promised that *Stockholm* would be made fully seaworthy within a hundred days at a cost of $900,000 (4.5 million Swedish krona), which was deemed a reasonable figure.

The work could begin immediately. An inspection team was organized, which included Captain Nordenson and officers from the various departments of the ship, to ensure that the repair work was done in conformity with the specifications. Simultaneously, preparations were being made for the trial, or more correctly, the groundwork was laid for the trial which everyone expected would begin soon.

Of course, from a public relations point of view, it would have been preferable for the two firms that owned the ships to reach an amicable settlement, but settlement attempts were stymied by the fear of loss of prestige. Captain Calamai had blamed *Stockholm* immediately. After that, it was impossible for Italian Line to take a different position. Captain Nordenson, on the other hand, had stated that he was unwilling to blame anyone and that fixing blame was up to the court. Even though the two shipowners had been in touch with each other at a very early stage to examine the possibilities for some kind of compromise, it became apparent that "the show must go on."

A big public relations war was under way in the United States. The Italian Line had engaged one of New York's leading firms early on to handle this phase of the matter. Eventually, Swedish America Line was obliged to respond in kind. Both parties were aware that the loser in the long run would be transatlantic passenger traffic. However, in the prevailing tense atmosphere, it was difficult to terminate the "war of words."

While all of this was going on, both parties sharpened their weapons for the preliminary hearing which was scheduled to begin in late summer in the United States District Court for the Southern District of New York. (Actually, most of the hearings were held at the New York County Lawyer's Association on Vesey Street, across the street from St. Paul's Chapel.) Carstens, of course, was the key witness for the Swedish side. What he said—or did not say—and how he conducted himself could be decisive on the question of liability and could also, at a possible future trial, have great consequences for Swedish America Line and its international reputation.

It was thus crucial for Swedish America Line's principal lawyer, Charles Haight, to prepare both Carstens and Captain Nordenson thoroughly prior to the scheduled hearing.

Carstens commented as follows about the preparations for the hearing:

People from the law firm picked me up at the Bethlehem Steel Shipyard in Brooklyn between eight and nine every morning and brought me back to the vessel at eight or nine every evening. We had long and intense internal 'hearings' at the law office.

Basically, I had to respond to the same questions, which the lawyers for Italian Line would be expected to ask me. We went through the nautical charts, bearings, and plotting—everything that had happened during the dramatic time I was on *Stockholm*'s bridge. We had the use of a room-sized enlargement of the chart. We checked different observation angles in order to ascertain *what* really had happened and *how* it could have happened. We went into great detail regarding the actions on the bridge of *Andrea Doria* and my own version of the navigation. We studied the construction of *Andrea Doria* thoroughly and had stability experts who examined blueprints and calculations.

Every day we received new information. Both Italian Line and Swedish America Line were, in principle, obliged to turn over all information about their respective ships. If they did not do so before the hearing, they knew the court would force them to do it later, or the court could refuse to admit evidence that had not been revealed before the hearing commenced.

In principle, too, both ships were to be available for inspection. As far as *Stockholm* was concerned, there was no problem—she was lying in Bethlehem Steel's drydock—and Italian Line personnel came from time to time to check on information they had received.

It was another matter with *Andrea Doria* lying on the bottom of the ocean. We did have her blueprints, stability calculations, and much more but were unable to check whether these agreed with reality. There were also good contacts with the Ansaldo Shipyard in Italy where *Andrea Doria* had been built and where the new Swedish America Line vessel *Gripsholm* was receiving her finishing touches. We knew the shipyard and Italian Line were not in complete agreement about *Andrea Doria's* construction and that both were concerned about their reputation if the preliminary hearing led to a full trial. This could be of great help to Swedish America Line. Even if *Andrea Doria* were no longer accessible, there was her sister ship, *Cristoforo Colombo,* which had gone into service one year later than *Andrea Doria* and was, as far as construction was concerned, an exact copy of *Andrea Doria.*

Naturally, Italian Line undertook the same detailed preparations in the United States, Italy, and Sweden. Her officers and crew had been flown home from New York immediately and had to attend, basically, the same kind of mock hearing in Genoa as did *Stockholm's* officers and crew in New York. They were trying to find gaps in Swedish America Line's story concerning, for example, equipment, speed in fog, manning of the bridge, and so on. Italian Line representatives, therefore, booked passage on *Kungsholm,* a Swedish America Line vessel which was to sail from New York on August 3, 1956. They planned to use interviews—or, rather, intimate conversations—with persons aboard to obtain information, especially about navigation, which could be used against Swedish America Line at the forthcoming hearing. However, who they were and what they were up to was soon apparent.

From the start, the tactic of Italian Line was to portray Captain Calamai as a navigator with long and extensive experience. Carstens, on the other hand, was to be presented to the court as an inexperienced youth. Carstens would be shown as being all alone on the bridge, in contrast to Captain Calamai, who had two mates with him on the bridge.

A law firm in Stockholm had been engaged by Italian Line to look into Carstens's past, presumably to ascertain whether there was anything unfavorable that might be used on cross-examination.

One day Carstens was picked up as usual at the Bethlehem Steel yard. When he arrived at the lawyers' office, he was told that he was to leave at once for a visit home. The ticket had already been purchased, and he was to be transported without delay to what is now John F. Kennedy International Airport for a flight to Copenhagen. Transatlantic flights were not common in those days, and the staff at the check-in counter probably thought Carstens was a most unusual passenger. All Carstens had with him was a briefcase, empty except for a couple of papers. They undoubtedly had never encountered anyone flying off to Europe without a suitcase full of shirts and other personal effects. He had strict instructions from the law firm to avoid talking with anyone who tried to talk with him. He was specifically cautioned not to talk to any journalists. He was to take the ferry from Copenhagen to Sweden as soon as possible and proceed to his home in Lund.

When the plane landed at Copenhagen's Kastrup Airport, Carstens was truly surprised. An ambulance and a large contingent of hospital personnel were waiting to meet the plane. Carstens thought that a passenger had taken ill during the flight, and his confusion was not diminished when he learned that all this activity was on his account. According to a message received by the manager of the Swedish America Line office in Copenhagen, Carstens was being sent home because of a nervous breakdown he had suffered in New York. This was not the case, of course, and the unnecessary alarm that had reached the airport had to be canceled. The ambulance and its personnel had to drive off, and the VIP room which had been reserved so Carstens could pass through unnoticed on his way to the ambulance was reopened for those for whom it was intended. When it was all over, Carstens was able to take a ferry over to Helsingborg, Sweden, and enjoy a good dinner with his father and brother-in-law.

Carstens many times has puzzled over this bizarre experience but never received a satisfactory explanation. It was clear the rumor that he was run-down and a nervous wreck had come from Sweden, but from whom? It certainly did not come from the Swedish America Line in Gothenburg. One can only speculate. It surely would have been a juicy tidbit for the Italian Line if Carstens had been picked up by an ambulance because of an alleged nervous breakdown. Only one party would have cause to gloat over the mental condition of such a key witness at the hearing scheduled to begin in a couple of weeks.

Carstens's stay in Sweden was mostly free from any great sensationalism. At home in Lund where Carstens lived, no one reacted to his sudden return from New York. He even met a few journalists whom he had known for years, but it never occurred to anybody to interview him.

In Gothenburg, however, the hunt was on for him. Naturally, the press had found out that he had left New York, and now the reporters wanted to know what possible reason there could be for such a sudden departure. The game of hide-and-seek with the media succeeded perfectly until the day Carstens was scheduled to travel from Lund to Gothenburg, the headquarters of Swed-

ish America Line, for a meeting with the personnel director, Henry Granberg. Then the fat was almost in the fire. When Carstens opened the door to Granberg's office, there sat a reporter from the *Gothenburg Weekly Journal* trying to convince Granberg to tell him where Carstens was.

Luckily, Granberg sized up the situation and said, "You'll have to wait or come back later." The reporter never associated the visitor in the office with the person he was pursuing for an interview. Carstens continued to evade the press with no further complications.

Now that Carstens was back home in Sweden, the directorate of the Swedish America Line naturally wanted to talk with him for firsthand information about the collision. Previously, all the company's information had come via long memos from the New York office and from the principal attorney, Charles Haight, an unusually skillful and sympathetic person, who had been of great help to Carstens during the whole time.

Carstens said:

When I was summoned to a meeting with Swedish America Line's president, Erik Wijk, I prepared myself very carefully. It was important to reply quickly and correctly to every question he asked.

As usual, there were a lot of security precautions, and sometimes, I wondered whether Swedish America Line harbored concern that I might disappear even here in Sweden. The journey from Lund up to Särö where Erik Wijk lived was via Halmstad, according to the instructions. There, using the name Körlin (the name of a technical inspector employed by the Broström concern), I was to check into a hotel. In the evening, "Körlin" was treated to a fine dinner, and the next morning, Wijk's chauffeur picked him up and drove him to Särö.

Naturally, it was an honor to be invited to the home of the company president. Erik Wijk's Villa Berghem had an unusually beautiful location in central Särö on a hill above the old church. At that time, a good part of the Broström dynasty lived in this area, most notably Ann-Ida Broström and shipowner Dan-Axel Broström.

The conversation with Erik Wijk turned out to be very pleasant and lasted nearly three hours. If Carstens had been worried that he was going to be given instructions pertaining to the forthcoming hearing, he was mistaken. Wijk just asked questions and listened very carefully to what Carstens had to say. As for the rest, Carstens was completely free to appear in court and testify. Carstens felt good having Wijk express that confidence in him.

After the visit to Erik Wijk, the time to return to New York was fast approaching. Carstens would much rather have stayed on in Sweden with his family, partly to get a longer perspective on what had happened but most of all to be present at the birth of his first child. However, he had to go back to New York again for the final "full dress rehearsal." The hearing was to begin on September 19 with Carstens appearing first in the witness box.

The return trip to New York was by air. When Carstens boarded the plane, it turned out that he was seated right in the midst of the members of *Andrea Doria*'s crew, who told him they were on their way to the hearing in New York. Of course, they did not know who Carstens was, and it was really important to keep a straight face and not reveal what he was up to. The Italians were very friendly and hospitable. They offered Carstens salami and wine. It must have come as something of a surprise for them when they met again a few days later in court in New York!

When Carstens returned to New York, life went on as usual until the hearing got under way. All the information was reviewed once again; the chart was checked from all possible angles, and new information, which had arrived while Carstens was away, was carefully analyzed. It was time for "the big match" to begin.

CHAPTER 15

Tough Pretrial Hearing in New York

As mentioned earlier, the *Lutine* bell is situated in the underwriting room of Lloyd's of London. As with other sea disasters, the bell was sounded after the loss of *Andrea Doria*. That act also engraved the name of the Italian luxury liner in the annals of great ships that have gone down. In the future, *Andrea Doria* would be named in the same category as *Titanic,* whose fate will likewise never be forgotten.

It seems that nothing captures the human imagination more than a major accident at sea. It is passed on in newspaper articles, books, and personal accounts from generation to generation. Major plane and train accidents, natural catastrophes, and calamities in industrial plants and mines are duly noted but tend to be soon forgotten, except, of course, for nuclear disasters.

The story of the collision between *Stockholm* and *Andrea Doria* and the resultant sinking of the Italian luxury liner belongs among the accounts of the greatest catastrophes at sea. However, it is not only the prolonged death throes of *Andrea Doria* that explain this phenomenon. Interest was am-

plified by the drawn-out proceedings in New York, in which neither party spared any effort to discredit the other. The first act of the drama was performed in the waters off Nantucket; the second act—the final act of the drama—took place in the handsome halls of the United States District Court for the Southern District of New York and the New York County Lawyers' Association.

The scheduled date, September 19, 1956, arrived, and the preliminary hearing convened. Carstens related:

> I felt like a well-trained boxer about to enter the ring. There had been many tough rounds of sparring. I had really gotten to test my strength with all kinds of imaginable opponents—lightweights and heavyweights, honorable fighters and those who hit below the belt. The lawyers for the Swedish America Line had spared no means to get me in shape and confront me with all the traps the opponents might employ. I had one standing order: "Tell the truth!" And answer in the same way time after time, even if the questions should be repeated in the cleverest wording. That was advice I really would have good use for in the days to come.

I didn't get a lot of sleep the night before the hearing. I was worried, even though I tried to tell myself that I had nothing to fear. On top of that, I had to listen to the noise of the ongoing repair work on *Stockholm,* so it felt almost like a liberation when Jan Ekman picked up Captain Nordenson and me at 9:00 A.M. to drive to the Federal Court, where in room 1506 and at the New York County Lawyers Association building, both in Manhattan, we were to be grilled day after day. We were prepared for that.

The "rules of the game" had been determined by Judge Lawrence E. Walsh, who had also decided when the hearing was to begin. Regarding the order in which the witnesses were to appear, he had assigned *Stockholm*'s mate on the bridge, Carstens, to be first, followed by the master of *Andrea Doria,* Captain Calamai, the responsible officer on the Italian ship's bridge.

Following the testimony of these witnesses, others involved from *Stockholm* and then *Andrea Doria* were to be heard: first Captain Nordenson, then *Andrea Doria*'s mates, *Stockholm*'s helmsman, and so on.

The order of testimony of the various witnesses had been predetermined. Carstens described his courtroom experience as follows:

Since I was first up in the witness stand, I was also like a "guinea pig." The general impression was probably that those who came after me would have it a little easier because they would have learned something about the methods of the judge and the attorneys.

Before I entered the witness box just after 10:00 A.M. on September 19, I was generally aware of the hearing rules that would apply. First, Swedish America Line's principal lawyer, Charles Haight, would begin with questions mainly dealing with navigation from the time I assumed the watch on the bridge of *Stockholm* at 8:30 P.M. on July 25, 1956, until the collision with *Andrea Doria.* I felt no uneasiness about that part of the hearing.

Following Haight would come the turn of Italian Line's principal lawyer, Eugene Underwood. He was renowned as a very tough lawyer—like Haight, one of the foremost maritime legal experts in the United States. Now the game would get rough. Underwood was not only a lawyer familiar with the art of squeezing the most unpleasant confessions out of his victims, but he was also an eminent actor.

As I had been warned, his interrogation could swing between almost demure friendliness to an explosive attack and arrogance, which could scare the life out of a witness. This was the man with whom I was to be confronted—I, who had never even seen the inside of a courtroom until now.

Following this anticipated major confrontation, I would be examined by a number of lawyers representing passenger and cargo plaintiffs. To these would be added experts in maritime law that both parties could throw into the fray if needed.

When we were just outside the courtroom, we were met by Italian Line's public relations people who were passing out a mimeographed sheet to everyone going in; it stated *Andrea Doria* was the innocent party in the collision. It was obvious the Italians were conducting their campaign on every possible level. The question was whether they were perhaps going too far by hammering in their message at any price and on every occasion.

Thus, the rules of the game had been laid down, although one could anticipate a good many surprises within that framework. What might the examination of witnesses deal with? Here too it was known in general how Swedish America Line and Italian Line witnesses would act, thanks to the complaint that had been filed which contained allegations and pronouncements.

Italian Line adamantly insisted *Andrea Doria* did not bear any blame for the accident. The company maintained that the two ships were on parallel courses and traveling in opposite directions; they would have passed each other starboard-to-starboard at a safe distance if *Stockholm* had not turned to starboard and rammed *Andrea Doria*.

Italian Line also stressed *Andrea Doria* was under the command of a captain of acknowledged skill who had two experienced mates with him on the bridge, both with captain's certificates. In contrast to this documented expertise, *Stockholm* had only one officer on the bridge at the time of the collision—an inexperienced young mate, according to Italian Line—while her captain was in his cabin. The bottom line was a claim against Swedish America Line for $30 million for the loss of *Andrea Doria*.

Swedish America Line in turn claimed $2 million from the Italian company—for repairs to *Stockholm* and for the loss of income from three canceled round-trip Atlantic crossings and one cruise.

Swedish America Line, which had been at a public relations disadvantage in the initial period following the collision, now mounted a major offensive to gain greater attention from the media, especially in the United States. It maintained the following ten points, which had been mentioned in the petition filed in court by Swedish America Line:

1. Those in command of *Andrea Doria* were careless, incompetent, and inattentive to their responsibilities.

2. *Andrea Doria* was not properly manned and equipped.

3. *Andrea Doria* neglected to keep a proper lookout.

4. *Andrea Doria* was traveling at a speed that was inappropriate and far too fast under the prevailing conditions.

5. The operation and/or maintenance of *Andrea Doria*'s radar equipment was inadequate.

6. *Andrea Doria* failed to give the signals mandated by international regulations for the prevailing conditions.

7. Suddenly and with no warning, *Andrea Doria* sheered straight across *Stockholm*'s course and collided with her.

8. *Andrea Doria* was maneuvered carelessly and inconsiderately.

9. *Andrea Doria* failed to stop or reverse her engines.

10. *Andrea Doria* neglected to take any adequate or appropriate measures to avoid collision with *Stockholm*.

These accusations were presented not only in court, but also at press conferences in both New York and Gothenburg, and they stirred up much attention.

One thing deserves mention: not with a single word did Swedish America Line comment on *Andrea Doria*'s stability or present any observation about why the ship sank. The company wanted to reserve this important piece of information for the preliminary hearing and the trial that might possibly ensue.

Of course, the preliminary hearing about the collision between *Stockholm* and *Andrea Doria* could not be compared with a real trial, but nevertheless, it attracted enormous attention. About fifty reporters from newspapers, magazines, radio, and television fought for space among the sixty-odd lawyers for the two shipping companies as well as a number of passengers, shippers, and charterers.

Captain Nordenson and Third Mate Carstens-Johannsen had been placed to the right in the courtroom. Following the introductory procedural questions, Carstens took his oath as a witness while *Andrea Doria*'s lawyers, experts, and public relations people glared threateningly at him.

Alvin Moscow, a reporter for the *Associated Press* who followed the entire proceedings and later published the book *Collision Course*, wrote: "The third mate of *Stockholm* seemed as nervous and unsure of himself as a lone longshoreman brought in to face the House of Lords."

Was that really the case? To this, Carstens replied:

It's obvious that my position was not entirely enviable. There I sat all alone in the witness box, totally exposed, not only to the opposing party's lawyers who would jump on every hesitation or uncertainty in my presentation, but also to the representatives of world journalism, who would interpret answers, or omit answers, as they pleased.

It was really fortunate that our own lawyer, Charles Haight, got to begin the hearing with me. That gave me a certain confidence in responding in front of this assemblage and in this environment, which was certainly different from anything I had previously experienced. Even before the hearing, I began to have a sense of what was going to happen.

Swedish America Line's lawyer maintained that an interpreter should be employed. Even though I was obviously rather comfortable using English, I did not and could not "think" in English. But the lawyer for the Italians, Eugene Underwood, jumped up immediately with objections to the use of an interpreter.

The lawyers for Italian Line used a system of mixing in terminology that would cause me unimaginable difficulty during examination involving a lot of technical terms and heated exchanges of words.

This acting game would occur innumerable times during the eleven days of my cross-examination. Probably, Underwood had anticipated that I would misunderstand the questions and give misleading responses. It could also have been a way to psyche me and undermine my self-confidence.

The result of this initial confrontation between the lawyers for Swedish America Line and Italian Line was that an interpreter could be used during my hearing. Captain Hjalmar Rothman was appointed. I also had Swedish stenographers who took down what I said in Swedish.

These stenographers had to be replaced many times during the hearing because of the demands of the job. It was nearly impos-

sible to hang in there when the lawyers came up with their running fire of objections, implications, and general babble. Finally, I asked someone with a tape recorder to sit behind the witness box and record the proceedings.

And so the second act of the play could begin with Eugene Underwood as the starring actor. He began his cross-examination with questions about my education and a kind of examination of my knowledge of navigational instruments. This all took an enormous amount of time, and the objective was obviously to try to prove that I was incompetent to be on the bridge of *Stockholm* on the night of the collision. Actually, I don't think he scored any major triumph, but, of course, I was personally involved.

Following this session, Underwood arrived at what actually happened at the time of the collision. What the lawyers for the Italian side had primarily devoted a lot of time and attention to was *Stockholm*'s course: the question of whether I had given the wrong command when I ordered hard to starboard just before the collision, whether there was or was not thick fog in the immediate area and, if so, how it would be possible to define "thick." Light, angles, distance, and maneuvering—Underwood interrogated me about all these things

The Italian team could claim a victory on the first day. One of the sixty-odd attorneys in the court had caught sight of Captain Nordenson and demanded that he be ordered out of the courtroom. The excuse for doing so was that Captain Nordenson might provide psychological support for me and that he might make use of what he heard during my testimony.

As usual, there was a lot of palaver. Haight protested, but this time he was overruled. The judge ordered Captain Nordenson to leave the room.

I really don't think anyone could produce a short, objective summary of my testimony during the eleven days it lasted. It was actually meaningless to carry on so long, since every day was by and large a repeat performance of what had happened during the interrogations of the previous day.

Of course, all those lawyers representing Italian Line, the cargo interests, or the passengers might occasionally have been able to score a point now and then, like when I could not immediately respond to their questions about *Stockholm*'s length, breadth, and turning radius. But on the whole, these were minor matters that had no significance with regard to the actual maneuvering.

As the hearing progressed, I began to feel more and more comfortable. Underwood's behavior from the outset made me angry, and I decided to match my strength with his. It really felt good when I saw that he got upset and had to enforce his argument by raising his voice even higher.

It's not surprising when a bomb goes off during a lengthy and arduous hearing. That happened while Underwood was questioning me about my duties and instructions as watch officer of the deck on *Stockholm*.

I thought I had accounted for everything: alert the captain in case of fog; never leave the bridge without a lookout; put the engine's telegraph on standby; check the lookout, navigation lights, and so on. In a voice unusually polite, Underwood asked whether I could remember any additional instructions.

When I was unable to immediately recall anything else, he reminded me that it was also the deck officer's responsibility to check the helmsman's steering. I had to admit that was the case.

As we went on, Underwood asked how often I checked out the helmsman, and I answered quite truthfully that it depended on who was presently at the helm. With regard to Peder Larsen, who was at the helm at the time of the collision, it was necessary to check him out more often because he was sometimes more interested in what was going on around him than in the actual steering.

A sigh went through the courtroom. The lawyers stood up, both Italian Line's and our own. This was totally unanticipated and totally unplanned.

The matter of helmsman Larsen had not come up during the postmortem discussions we had every evening following the day's hearing. That's why what I had just said came as a shock to our attorneys and as a long-awaited triumph for our opponents,

who thought they had broken through our defense.

Every evening we had a thorough review of what had gone on during the day. Attorney Haight, for obvious reasons, was not exactly pleased with what I had just said, but he opined that it could hardly injure anyone providing that helmsman Larsen didn't say anything to the contrary.

When he turned up at the hearing and was asked about his qualifications as a helmsman, Larsen said that he steered like a little old lady. Yet, deviations from the course had been minimal and had no significance whatever in connection with the collision.

The case of helmsman Larsen received a lot of attention in the media. The lawyers for the Italian Line tried to exploit it to the breaking point, but many others accepted my spontaneous testimony as evidence that we were all telling the truth, even though that might not gain us a momentary advantage.

Today, as I look back on the testimony regarding helmsman Larsen, I reckon we will never get past his whimsical steering of *Stockholm*. The course records from both ships, which eventually appeared during the hearing, proved with all desirable clarity that Larsen indeed steered the prescribed course, but occasionally in a zigzag pattern. That would surely have been exploited by the lawyers for the Italian Line, even if I had said nothing.

After eleven days and around sixty hours of testimony, my trial was over. Italian Line's lawyers had been rough on me, trying to get me mentally off balance and physically tired. Yet, as the days went by, I thought things got easier. I had become accustomed to the surroundings and gotten the hang of the hearing technique.

The lawyers for Italian Line and the freight and passenger interests got nowhere. The questions were the same day after day, even if in different versions. Underwood's outbursts had largely lost their intensity. The news reporters began to get used to them; after all, his theatrics were partly for their benefit. On me, they no longer had any effect. I could very well have gone on for another eleven days.

Sometimes when the lawyers really got to wrangling, I was ordered to leave the hearing room so I wouldn't hear what they were saying. But nobody realized there were loudspeakers outside, so I heard everything. When I asked why I was being "banished," the judge said they wanted to confer without my listening in. Then I said, to the amusement of all, "Then you'd better turn off the loudspeakers!"

When my testimony began, a lot of people figured it would be wrapped up in a couple of days. Why did it drag on so long? There have been a lot of theories, but I think one is pretty reasonable. The Italian company wanted to keep *Andrea Doria*'s Captain Calamai out of the witness box at all costs until the baseball World Series got underway in New York because then all the negative publicity that Captain Calamai's testimony might create would be drowned out by the clamor of the games. This was indirectly corroborated by the Italian public relations people.

How did independent observers evaluate Carstens's testimony? On the whole, very positively. Among the shelves full of media clippings, there were only a few unfavorable comments about Carstens. Three quotations from papers whose reporters attended the entire hearing reflected the tenor of the journalistic point of view. In the Swedish weekly magazine *SE*, Ulf Nilsson wrote the following:

There is no doubt that Carstens-Johannsen handled himself well. The banner headlines about his alleged mistakes more likely served to conceal the fact that the hearing did not offer any sensational developments. Instead, people became increasingly impressed by the Swede. "He must be telling the truth," say the experts. "It's impossible to lie so long and in the face of such questions. We haven't been able to catch him in the least little hint of a self-contradiction. And a clever lawyer like Eugene Underwood could always find loopholes, if there had been any."

As far as *Andrea Doria*'s company was concerned, the cross-examination ended with something seriously resembling resig-

nation. They had gathered some ammunition for the summations, but they had not proven a single, legally valid accusation. It is not a crime to be young and inexperienced.

The well-known radio commentator Arne Thorén wrote the following in the *Weekly Journal (Veckjournalen):*

When Eugene Underwood had finished his long examination, perhaps the most important question remained unanswered: Why did *Andrea Doria* turn to port just a few minutes before the catastrophe? According to Carstens-Johannsen's testimony, that maneuver caused the accident. Underwood devoted a couple of days to finding a crack in Carstens's defense on this point but in vain. Over and over, the mate accounted for virtually every second of the minutes around 11:00 P.M. on the night of the accident, and over and over again he showed himself to be a witness of rarely seen character. He was never close to contradicting himself; he could stand for every syllable of what he was saying and had said. And this despite being severely handicapped by the Swedish interpreter's difficulties in translating the lawyer's questions and his own answers."

Finally, in a summary of a major review article in which the *New York Herald Tribune* presented its outlook on the hearing with Carstens, the paper pointed out among other things that the third mate of *Stockholm* stayed as calm and "wrinkle-proof" as his dapper dark blue uniform. He was the only witness thus far, and the cross-examination had been very rough. But, stressed the paper, although the lawyers had so far repeatedly gone over what had happened, they had not been able to shake the witness or contradict the essential features of his testimony. The *Tribune* further reported that Carstens's testimony had been given in a sincere and forthright manner that left the impression he was trying to be helpful.

One of the lawyers actually said in the courtroom that he was trying to prove the young third mate was incompetent to navigate a ship as large as *Stockholm*. If that upset the witness, he showed no sign of it, according to the *Tribune*.

Carstens summarized:

My testimony was over—an interesting but also unpleasant experience. I don't dream about it, but I wouldn't like to go through it again. I don't really know how things might have turned out if I hadn't had Charles Haight at my side the whole time—a quiet, self-possessed lawyer, very courteous but unrelentingly dogged in his interrogation. He had perfected the art of interrupting the other side's lawyers at exactly the right time and giving me time to think.

He acted like a true friend outside the courtroom, too, not only to me, but to my family as well. He continually kept them informed by both telegrams and letters. We also stayed in touch for many years after the hearing in New York, until his death some years ago.

The second of the witnesses was Captain Calamai. Between the day of the collision and the time of the preliminary hearing, he had been back in Italy. Together with his mates, he had gone through what had happened on the bridge and prepared his defense. Upon his return to New York, the word was that while in Italy, he had been admitted to a hospital.

Carstens said:

The only time I found myself in the presence of Captain Calamai, except for when I could see into *Andrea Doria*'s bridge when we collided, was when he was gong to replace me in the witness box. What do you say at such a moment? I couldn't say, "Glad to meet you." In the first place, it wouldn't be true, and in the second place, it might have been perceived as a provocation, so I just said, "How do you do?"

In the tense situation that prevailed, I couldn't expect a friendly reply, of course. But Captain Calamai said nothing. He just glared at me. Yes, glared, just as if he were thinking, "There's the man who sank my ship."

Of course, I had no guilt feelings, but just during that brief encounter with *Andrea Doria*'s captain, I really felt sorry for him. He had lost his ship through an unexplainable maneuver, and now he was going to sit in the witness box and probably be grilled as roughly as I had been. And he really had very little room in which to maneuver. Italian Line's public relations people had already distributed to the press a written memo that described what Captain Calamai was going to say at the hearing. He had to go along with it, whether he wanted to or not.

I had received Captain Nordenson's permission to attend the hearing as it went on, and I took full advantage of it. During the first part, when Italian Line's principal attorney Eugene Underwood was in charge of the interrogation, nothing essential happened. Everything had been prearranged and followed the communiqué that had been handed out in detail.

So Captain Calamai adamantly refuted my and Swedish America Line's version of the collision and the two ships' relative positions. According to Captain Calamai, *Stockholm* came up on *Andrea Doria*'s starboard side in foggy weather. There was no risk of a collision, and the change of course to port on *Andrea Doria*'s bridge was intended simply to increase the distance between the two ships.

In every detail, Underwood's examination of Captain Calamai presented an inverse picture of what had come out during my hearing. Captain Calamai spoke in a low voice, but he didn't hesitate when responding to Underwood's carefully prepared questions. The translation from Italian into English was handled by Joseph Ivancich, an American who had formerly been a pilot on the Suez Canal.

Underwood hammered away at the fact that Captain Calamai, two mates with captain's certificates, and two lookouts were on the bridge. In the attempt to portray *Andrea Doria* as a safe ship, there was included a comprehensive description of all the navigation equipment she had on board. Quite simply, he presented a picture of an exceptional ship under very competent command.

Underwood skillfully piloted Captain Calamai past all the pitfalls, and during this stage of the hearing, the press was unable to report any surprises. But they would come later during the hearing.

The chief attorney for Swedish America Line, Charles Haight, opened his interrogation with questions about the use of the navigational equipment on board *Andrea Doria*. Haight's questioning of Captain Calamai was done at an entirely different tempo and tone from that which Underwood used when I was being interrogated. That certainly created good will for Swedish America Line among everyone involved.

No one doubted *Andrea Doria* was a technically well-equipped ship, but the question was whether the people in charge on the bridge could make use of all that instrumentation.

To Haight's first main question—whether Captain Calamai himself had any special training in radar technology—the answer was "no." The captain also had to acknowledge that one of the mates lacked such training as well and that no one on the bridge had plotted the radar observations of the approaching ship. The explanation was that "the ships were on parallel courses, and thus there was no need for plotting." The plotting table had not even been taken out on the night in question.

But the question that attracted the greatest attention during the interrogation of Captain Calamai dealt with the missing logbooks. These included the bridge, engine room, and radio logbooks. Before the preliminary hearing got underway, it had been stipulated that both companies were to exchange significant documents in order to simplify the proceedings, and then it turned out that only quite unimportant documents pertaining to the actual navigation had been saved when *Andrea Doria* went to the bottom. On the other hand, Captain Calamai had personally taken secret documents from *Andrea Doria* pertaining to the Atlantic Pact. That strengthened earlier suspicions *Andrea Doria* was a NATO vessel, built as a troop transport and even financed by certain American interests. After the collision, it appeared that she did not measure up to the calculations either for a passenger liner or for a troop transport.

How the logbooks had come to be left on *Andrea Doria* was never really cleared up, and Captain Calamai said that he first realized they were still on the bridge only after he had left the ship. Calamai first stated that he had given a general order to save the logbooks and they were supposed to have been taken care of by an officer candidate. Later it was learned that only the NATO volumes had been saved.

There is no doubt that Captain Calamai had landed in a precarious situation, inasmuch as Italian law required the commander of a sinking ship to save all logbooks before leaving her.

Haight's examination of *Andrea Doria*'s master turned often on the missing logbooks and the disorder on the bridge when it became clear the ship might sink. Logbooks and marine charts could have greatly contributed to the possibility of reconstructing *Andrea Doria*'s course prior to the collision. And now it was said that everything had gone to the bottom. But was that really so?

Questioning concerning the missing logbooks continued, and representatives of Italian Line in New York suddenly announced they had been sent to Italy to be examined along with other papers.

As to this, Carstens stated:

There's a lot to suggest that this statement was correct, that all the valuable papers were sent to Italy, and that they constituted important material for the mock trial the Italian Line held there before the preliminary hearing got underway in New York.

Charles Haight brought up the problem of the missing logbooks from time to time, trying to find a loophole in Captain Calamai's defense. Suddenly, a ship's journal turned up. When it became perfectly obvious that it had been taken apart and fastened together again—which is absolutely forbidden—Swedish America Line's lawyer inquired about this in great detail.

Attorney Underwood protested vehemently. After a heated dispute between the two attorneys, the judge ruled that Captain Calamai should reply to the question of whether there had been any damage to the logbook's cover and contents.

This ruling prompted a great spectacle in the courtroom. Attorney Underwood persisted in his protest, took the journal from Captain Calamai, and looked as if he were going to examine it. Then he raised it over his head and twisted at it until the pages flew all over the floor. The seal that by law should not be broken fell apart, and thus any evidence the logbook had been tampered with was destroyed.

Attorney Underwood had achieved his aim, but he'd hardly increased confidence in Captain Calamai and Italian Line.

Charles Haight devoted a good deal of his interrogation of Captain Calamai to the fact that although *Andrea Doria* had been in thick fog for a long time, she was running at almost full speed. That action was contrary to international regulations, even though it was no secret they were often not followed. But in a hearing where it was important to establish what measures had been taken or not taken to avoid the collision, the ship's speed was very important and might have great significance for the outcome of the case in a possible subsequent trial.

A lot of attention was also paid to *Andrea Doria*'s stability and her captain's actions to save her. But the answers to the questions posed were very evasive and mainly limited to "I don't know" or "I don't remember."

The most dramatic moment during the entire hearing came when Captain Calamai, over the protests of Underwood, was ordered by the judge to describe the crucial distances and bearings when *Stockholm* was observed before the collision. From this, it was clear the two ships were not, as had been previously asserted, on parallel courses but on courses that would lead to a collision.

In a courtroom where one could hear a pin drop, Captain Calamai admitted in a very low voice: "I can see that now."

Four pertinent facts had emerged from the examination of *Andrea Doria*'s captain:

1. It was Captain Calamai's fault that the ship was traveling too fast in the fog.

2. Calamai had not plotted the radar displays and, therefore, did not know *Andrea Doria* was on a collision course.

3. In contradiction to rules of the road at sea, *Andrea Doria* had turned in the wrong direction when a collision was imminent.

4. The captain was unfamiliar with *Andrea Doria*'s stability problem and had made no attempt to correct the ship's obvious list following the collision.

When the mates of *Andrea Doria* eventually appeared in court, the cross-examination dealt largely with courses, plotting, and the risk of collision. Second Mate Curzio Franchini, constantly pressured by attorney Haight, tried as long as he could to avoid answering the question of how he would have navigated during the minutes before the collision if Piero Calamai had not been on the bridge. Franchini said that his answer might be interpreted as a criticism of his captain and the maneuvers he had made. At Haight's insistence, the answer finally came: "Theoretically, I would probably have ordered reverse engines and turned in the other direction."

Haight then asked the witness: "In which direction would you have turned?"

"Probably to starboard—to the right."

Swedish America Line's attorney had finally received the answer he had so long desired.

Stockholm's Captain Nordenson was the third witness to appear at the preliminary hearing. Like Captain Calamai, he was a mariner of the old breed, an honorable man who scorned untruthfulness. During the years following his retirement, the captain often referred to the collision with *Andrea Doria*. Carstens got the impression that however he sought to forget that terrible night with all its horrors, it pursued him for the rest of his life. It would be strange if it had been otherwise. He constantly professed his and Carstens's innocence and believed that both of them had acted appropriately. Yet, the memory lived on, and he often asked why fate could not have spared him that appalling tragedy off Nantucket.

Nordenson also spoke frequently about the arduous hearing and how he had experienced it. He described how the Italian lawyers, experts, and public relations men glowered at him until he began to feel depressed and generally uncertain.

Often during the trial, Underwood's questions of witnesses from *Stockholm* were cleverly formulated, and they required some reflection by the witness. On these occasions, people on the Italian side stood and began to measure the time with chronometers. It was these annoying tactics that plagued Captain Nordenson, not the factual content of the questions.

Undoubtedly, one of the major problems for Captain Nordenson was that he had not been on the bridge at the moment of the collision. But many years later, he spoke about the catastrophe as though he had actually been there and experienced every phase of what went on. This showed that, having subsequently acquainted himself with every detail of what had gone on, he approved of the actions taken by his third mate.

There is no question that Captain Nordenson was not in peak condition when his examination began on October 22. The catastrophe off Nantucket hit the sixty-three-year-old captain hard, and the pressures on him continued upon his arrival in New York when he was overwhelmed by questions from the mass media. Then began the long preparations for the preliminary hearing, even as he wanted to monitor the repair work on *Stockholm* at Bethlehem Steel.

In accordance with the schedule agreed upon, Swedish America Line's attorney

Charles Haight quizzed Captain Nordenson first. Two central questions came up immediately. The first was with regard to Carstens being in sole charge on the bridge; the other was whether or not *Stockholm* found herself in the wrong lane according to an agreement among steamship companies that serviced the North Atlantic. (According to this agreement, ships of signatory nations destined for Europe from New York would sail about 20 nautical miles farther south than *Stockholm* did, while vessels traveling in the opposite direction would pass *Nantucket* lightship at a distance of only a couple of miles. [Sweden had *not* signed this agreement.])

With regard to Third Mate Carstens-Johannsen, Captain Nordenson made it clear that he had absolute confidence in him and in the way he maneuvered *Stockholm*.

Regarding whether the Swedish ship found herself in a lane intended for traffic into New York, Captain Nordenson pointed out that in his opinion, it was safer in this heavily trafficked area to approach another ship head-on, or bow-to-bow, rather than on intersecting courses.

On the second day, Underwood brought up the same question. It came as something of a shock in the courtroom when he presented a document that had been inserted into the Swedish National Maritime Administration's publication, *Information Concerning Seafaring*. This document read as follows: "According to an advisory from the National Board of Trade, ships of the following companies shall follow the routes across the North Atlantic described in *Pilot Charts* published by the American Hydrographic Office [the source of the 'southern' route mentioned earlier]." Swedish America Line was listed as one of the signatories of this document.

Captain Nordenson replied that he knew nothing about this agreement. Underwood's objective was probably to create confusion and make *Stockholm's* commander feel uncertain. The principal attorney for Italian Line knew, or should have known, that neither Swedish America Line nor *Andrea Doria's* owner, Italian Line, had signed any document concerning prescribed lanes for eastbound and westbound traffic.

The accepted practice at a hearing was that documents the parties proposed to refer to would be listed in the courtroom in the presence of the lawyers of both parties. But this topic had not been listed and hence the impression was amplified that an attempt was being made to intimidate *Stockholm's* captain. Subsequent contacts with Sweden confirmed that Swedish America Line had never signed the document presented by Underwood or recommended that its ships leaving New York should follow a more southerly route.

What many people had feared occurred on the third day of Captain Nordenson's testimony. Underwood asked how long it would take before *Stockholm* and *Andrea Doria* would meet if they had a combined speed of 40 knots and were positioned at a distance of 10 nautical miles from each other.

Once that question had been asked, Leonard Matteson, who was handling claims for cargo loss and damage against both the Swedish and Italian companies, started his chronometer and stared challengingly at Nordenson.

This persistent psychological harassment was too much for Captain Nordenson, who collapsed. Accompanied as usual by protests from the opposing party, the hearing was interrupted. Nordenson was conveyed to St. Luke's Hospital, where the doctors certified a possible minor thrombosis of the brain, i.e., a stoppage in one of the brain's capillary vessels.

But Underwood did not give up so easily. He publicly insinuated that Captain Nordenson had only "played sick" in order to escape unpleasant questions during the hearing.

To put a stop to this allegation, which was eagerly disseminated by Italian Line's public relations people, the judge decided to have two distinguished specialists examine Captain Nordenson. Following exhaustive tests, they arrived at the same conclusion as the hospital's own doctors and thus silenced the defamation campaign.

After four weeks in the hospital, Captain Nordenson was so much better that he was able to begin a fourteen-day convalescence, accompanied by his wife, in a lovely house north of New York which had been placed at their disposal by one of Swedish America Line's most loyal cruise passengers.

Captain Nordenson's testimony resumed on December 3 and was to be limited to morning sessions. The interrogation could also be broken off if Captain Nordenson felt tired. But just a few days later, the court announced that the hearing was to be postponed until after New Year's. Nothing new had emerged, but the initiated knew even then that the preliminary hearing on the collision between *Stockholm* and *Andrea Doria* was nearing an end.

Of course, Captain Nordenson wanted to go home and celebrate Christmas in Sweden, but there was no way he could go home. His examination had only been delayed, and he was therefore not allowed to leave the United States unless the Swedish America Line could post security of about 150 million Swedish krona. So instead of celebrating Christmas in Sweden, Captain Nordenson and his wife spent the holiday in balmy sunshine on the Gulf of Mexico.

Carstens never signed off *Stockholm* after her arrival in New York; he officially served the whole time as third mate and lived on board.

With Captain Nordenson's permission, Carstens attended the testimony of subsequent witnesses. After all, this was a legal proceeding on the highest level, and his primary interest was in how his comrades on *Stockholm*—mates, engine room personnel, helmsmen, and lookouts—would handle themselves.

As to this, Carstens commented:

I thought even then that everyone did very well. Now that I have had occasion to study the confidential reports Swedish America Line's office in Gothenburg received from the attorneys in New York, I see that my judgment at that time, however subjective, was shared by Swedish America Line's management. The appreciative words concerning the eighteen-year-old lookout Sten Johansson were particularly gratifying. I fully agreed with Swedish America Line when they designated him as "a very valuable witness." From his vantage point high above anyone else's, he had the exclusive advantage of seeing what nobody else saw.

In spite of all the attention shown by attorney Haight, his colleagues, my personal friend Jan Ekman, and all the families, it still felt great—almost liberating, in fact—to stand once again on *Stockholm*'s bridge after the repairs were completed. Before us, we had one cruise to the West Indies and one to Bermuda. In addition, I was "expecting," so to speak. And on November 16 came the news: It was a girl! More than one mug was hoisted to celebrate the event.

On December 8, we were once again to begin the trip to Gothenburg and Copenhagen that had been so dramatically interrupted off Nantucket on July 25.

The preliminary hearing in New York was still going on, but for me, it was just a memory. Now we were sailing as a "Christmas boat" to Scandinavia, and the ship was full of eager passengers who were going to observe the greatest celebration of the year in the old country.

Personally, I was really full of anticipation and delight about getting home to Sweden after all these months of inquiries and, most of all, uniting with my wife, Liliane, and seeing my newborn daughter for the first time.

The interrupted hearing got underway again in early January 1957 with a less brusque Eugene Underwood. A couple of days later, Captain Nordenson terminated his participation with the following words: "I know that you blame Carstens-Johannsen for being young, and you have also called him inexperienced. You might call him inexperienced in comparison with my experience of nearly forty-six years at sea, but on the other hand, there is a difference between inexperience and incompetence. As far as I can see, he demonstrated no incompetence in his handling of the ship."

On January 25, 1957, Captain Nordenson and his wife were finally able to travel home to Sweden; the news of a settlement had become official the day before. He placed particular value on one welcoming greeting and spoke about it often: Ann-Ida Broström had sent a floral arrangement and a letter in which she expressed her admiration for Gunnar Nordenson, captain of *Stockholm*.

After all, *Stockholm* could be considered to be "hers." She was the ship's "godmother" and had christened her with the following words: "May good fortune and prosperity follow you across the seas, and may you be beneficial to humanity and an honor to our country."

CHAPTER 16

Agreement Reached: *Andrea Doria* Accepts Liability

The preliminary hearing investigating the collision between *Stockholm* and *Andrea Doria* on the night of July 25 and 26, 1956, was formally brought to an end on January 24, 1957. It had consumed a lot of time, much more than many had envisioned, but now it was all over and the two companies involved, Italian Line and Swedish America Line, had reached an agreement.

Judge Lawrence S. Walsh was justified in congratulating the two parties on reaching an out-of-court settlement. The media, which had followed the hearing with unflagging interest in order to describe the world's greatest ever maritime drama (at least in terms of money), had to call it a day.

But questions remained. Who had won? Who had lost? Who was to blame? Who was without fault? Why did the "unsinkable" *Andrea Doria* go to the bottom? The answers might surface in the future, but not just then. For the companies involved, this meant that the truth was hidden in the price of the agreement.

But there were winners. For example, the insurance companies had to pay the shipowners' losses no matter who was to blame, but additional hearings or a trial would mean more attorneys' fees as well.

And passenger lines in general—not only Italian Line and Swedish America Line, but every shipowner who transported passengers across the sea—could heave a sigh of relief that people would not be reminded daily of the hazards of crossing the oceans.

The end of the preliminary hearing came abruptly for those not intimately involved. For the management and attorneys of Swedish America Line, it was a logical result of what had gone on previously. It was surely not unanticipated by Italian Line, which had been confronted with a long list of accusations during the course of the hearing.

The collision off Nantucket had attracted so much attention in the United States that the House of Representatives immediately appointed the Bonner Committee (named for its chairman), and charged it with investigating the extent to which *Andrea Doria* had fulfilled the requirements for watertight compartments and stability laid down by the 1948 Safety of Life at Sea Convention (SOLAS).

The committee presented its report, based partially on analyses by the Ansaldo Shipyard, in December 1956. In brief, it reached the following conclusions:

> *Andrea Doria* just barely met the specifications of the SOLAS convention for the distribution of watertight bulkheads. The report on stability indicated the ship could also meet the requirements of the convention, but on condition that she was ballasted with rather large and specific amounts of liquid in the various tanks.
>
> It is impossible to explain why *Andrea Doria* sank after the collision on July 25, 1956, other than to accept that on that occasion she was not properly ballasted in accordance with the convention, and that there were errors in her design and construction.

It was the committee's judgment that at the time of the collision, *Andrea Doria* was only one-third as stable as she should have been.

The report was a hard blow for the Italian company. Suddenly, interest shifted away from the collision and how it had come about. Now the question was why did *Andrea Doria* sink?

The engineers on the Italian ship might have been able to answer that question. They had been scheduled to appear in the witness box in mid-January 1957.

Fortified by the Bonner Committee's report and prior to the cross-examination of *Andrea Doria*'s engineers, Swedish America Line had requested documents pertaining to ballasting, piping systems, and other data concerning the ship's stability. All of this material, found in twenty-six different books and reports, was submitted to the court on January 8, 1957, but the hearing was terminated before the engineers on *Andrea Doria* could tell the court what had gone on in the ship's engine and generator rooms.

Some six thousand pages of testimony had been presented by witnesses during the four months the case had gone on. The lawyers, technicians, and management of both companies involved had carefully scrutinized every single line.

At regular intervals, Swedish America Line in Gothenburg received thick envelopes containing not only the transcripts of testimony, but also comments on what the witnesses had said and not said, the way they conducted themselves before the court, and so on. Broström's technical division paid particular attention to everything that had to do with *Andrea Doria*'s stability. One of the world's foremost experts in this field, Professor C. W. Prohaska of Copenhagen, was contacted at an early stage, and he contributed ongoing calculations as the reports flowed in.

The underwriters in London gained simultaneous access to all the documents and thus came to serve as a kind of "jury" in the trial which was not a trial.

From the unenviable position of those who would have to pay no matter how the case concluded, the underwriters could determine when the parties might be ready to agree on a compromise.

From the outset, of course, it was in the interests of both Swedish America Line and Italian Line to make short shrift of the proceedings. But there was a catch: a possible compromise must not be so formulated as to indicate blame.

The lawyers for both the Swedish and the Italian companies had met at the beginning of August, two weeks after the collision, to sound out the possibilities of an agreement. The meeting proved, however, that the prerequisites for such an agreement were not at hand just then.

Another meeting took place in Copenhagen on August 24, 1956. On the one side were Dr. Manzitti, Chairman of Finmare (which had economic control of Italian

Line) and the Italian company's Vice President Donini. On the other side were Erik Wijk, president of Swedish America Line, and Fritjof Nordborg, the director of Broström's legal department.

Once again, the Italians showed great interest in reaching some sort of agreement, but Wijk, who had already begun to feel confident about his company's position, maintained that it was pointless to talk about a compromise prior to the hearing scheduled to begin on September 19. The result was an agreement to meet again in London when all the evidence had been taken. Then the whole question would be addressed anew.

As previously mentioned, the English underwriters for both sides were extremely anxious to reach an agreement as quickly as possible. Otherwise, the legal expenses were going to be an enormous burden. Had the proceedings gone as far as a formal trial, it was estimated the costs would amount to something like $3.5 million.

Even before the testimony of the witnesses had been completed (a stipulation of the Copenhagen agreement), the English underwriters proposed a meeting in London to seek a settlement. Swedish America Line and the Swedish Steamship Underwriters AB concluded they would not hold out against the proposal, and a meeting in London was scheduled for January 8, 1957.

Much had happened between the first meeting in Copenhagen in early August 1956 and the announcement of the 1957 London meeting. Developments had pretty much favored Swedish America Line. The investigations in Italy, especially those at the Ansaldo Shipyard, had produced valuable information, and the Bonner Committee report had arrived at an opportune moment for the Swedish company. In addition, after much insistence from *Stockholm*'s attorney, the material needed to make an exact estimate of *Andrea Doria*'s stability had

finally been delivered to the court. Swedish America Line had received a categorical statement by cable from the United States that if there were to be a trial, the proportional fault rule would be applied by the American court.

This piece of information was unusually important. It was then the rule in the United States that if both vessels were found to be at fault, the damages would be divided between them equally, even in cases where the proportion of blame might reasonably have been 75 percent and 25 percent, for example. The reason the U.S. court decided to proceed differently in this particular case was because it involved a collision between two non-American ships in international waters. Both Italy and Sweden were signatories to the 1910 Collision Convention, which provided for proportional fault.

After what had already been revealed during the preliminary hearing, and faced with the obvious risk of being found more to blame than Swedish America Line in a potential trial, the Italian Line and its principal owner, the Italian government, were very concerned. In the current situation, it was undeniably more advantageous to accept an out-of-court settlement, one not entered into the public record, than to be found at fault by a court.

The London meeting that took place in early January 1957, decided the matter. With the participation of the English underwriters, Swedish America Line and Italian Line were able to reach an agreement which in one stroke swept under the carpet questions of international rules of the road, proper distribution of watertight bulkheads, and stability calculations. When two cars are damaged in a collision, the matter frequently winds up in court, even if no personal injuries are involved. Yet in this case involving fifty-six deaths and millions of dollars in material damages, including the loss of one of the world's finest passenger ships, no court decision would be forthcoming.

Many meetings and discussions had taken place prior to the decisive meeting in London among all the parties involved. So, for example, President Erik Wijk of Swedish America Line and Director Carl-E Åhmansson and Captain Gustaf Ahrne of the Swedish Protection and Indemnity Association met with Paul Worseley, claims expert with the Willis Faber brokerage firm, who had been kept continually updated on the stability of *Andrea Doria* and on what settlement might be deemed reasonable as the reports flowed in.

On January 8, 1957, Cyril Miller held a dinner party. He was one of the top people in the United Kingdom Mutual Steamship Insurance Association Ltd., which represented a number of protection and indemnity (marine liability) insurers, the so-called "P and I clubs." Both Swedish and Italian representatives, as well as a number of important underwriters, were invited. The idea was to try to create an agreeable atmosphere for the imminent, conclusive negotiations. According to one of the guests, the evening passed just as the host had hoped. If an outsider unfamiliar with the real purpose for the dinner had been present, he would hardly have been able to imagine that he was among antagonists who would argue against each other the next day in difficult negotiations and would come to an agreement following one of the greatest maritime disasters in the history of the world.

On the following morning, the group gathered at the Savoy Hotel: Finmare's board chairman, Dr. Manzitti; Italian Line's attorney, Dr. Francesco Berlingieri, who had attended the hearing in New York; Swedish America Line's president, Erik Wijk; and Broström's senior attorney, Fritjof Nordborg.

Wijk immediately put forward his proposal for a settlement in which each party would be responsible for its own damages as well as for compensation of passengers and cargo on its own ship.

This was a stiff proposal for Italian Line, so Wijk referred to the recently released Bonner Committee report and to a cable from New York concerning the result of an initial processing of the newly arrived and conclusive material on *Andrea Doria*'s stability. Still, the Italians responded at once that they could not, under any circumstances, agree to such a proposal.

Offer followed counteroffer in the difficult negotiations. Later in the day, a meeting took place in Cyril Miller's office among the people who had been present at the dinner on the previous evening. In addition, another American maritime lawyer, William Symmers, had been summoned. Wijk repeated his proposal for a settlement, and Miller floated a compromise to the parties that Wijk could accept, although somewhat reluctantly.

The final meeting was held in Miller's office on the following day. All of those previously mentioned were present, along with three prominent underwriters. For their part, the underwriters said they had originally contemplated a settlement according to the 50-50 principle, but now, in the prevailing circumstances, they could also consider an agreement along the lines suggested by Wijk and Miller.

Wijk, an experienced negotiator with much testimony in his favor, made a final demand that the insurance companies also cover Swedish America Line's lost revenues and other costs not recoverable under the terms of *Stockholm*'s insurance. The underwriters objected, but since they were also under heavy pressure to avoid a drawn-out trial at almost any cost, they eventually met Wijk halfway. Swedish American Line would receive compensation outside the terms of insurance for a sum of up to $200,000 but would have to shoulder its revenue losses.

In its final form the settlement, for the most part, satisfied Swedish America Line's demands. Briefly, it stated that each company would be responsible for damages in respect of its own ship, i.e., Italian Line for the loss of *Andrea Doria* and Swedish America Line for repairs to *Stockholm*'s bow. The settlement also called for the parties involved to cooperate in coming to a speedy agreement with all those who in many different ways had been affected by the collision. This aspect might involve such things as compensation to the survivors and the injured as well as coverage for the cost of luggage or cargo losses. A special fund was to be established for this purpose. Any monies remaining in this fund after all damages had been paid would accrue to *Andrea Doria*'s hull insurance underwriters.

For all practical purposes, the settlement would be complete when all of the parties involved in London had given their approval. However, the representatives of the Italian Line requested four to five days to think the matter over and to allow them to secure the Italian underwriters' agreement.

While waiting for the agreement to be signed, Italian Line's attorneys requested a one-week postponement of the examination of witnesses in New York. Swedish America Line's senior attorney at the proceedings, Charles Haight, was instructed by cable not to oppose such a postponement.

There was a hitch in the settlement. It had been reached among the principal interests of Swedish America Line and Italian Line, but there was no similar understanding concerning other involved parties, such as the passengers and the cargo interests. The London compromise had not made specific provisions for them. According to the agreement, both Swedish America Line and Italian Line would commit themselves to cooperating to adjust any "third-party" claims for compensation as soon as possible.

Fritjof Nordborg, then the director of Broström's legal department, wrote the following confidential memorandum to Swedish America Line's management regarding such claims and the problems concerning them:

The limitation period for such claims is two years. If the case is recalled from the federal court, where it would otherwise be heard, before the claims have been paid and hence liquidated, these innocent parties [outside interests or third parties] could bring suit against the companies in some state court. That would involve losing the advantage of having bound all procedural matters to the federal court which now has the petitions from the companies.

It can be added that the judge in charge of the hearing of witnesses had set February 15, 1957, as the last day for submitting claims. If the third-party plaintiffs, either the passengers or the cargo interests, could show due cause, however, a further extension could be granted.

However, it was absolutely critical that the settlement reached by the two companies be kept secret, at least until February 15.

The overriding consideration of the London settlement between Italian Line and Swedish America Line (with the participation of the insurers involved) was that no winner or loser would be singled out. Nevertheless, the terms did just that!

On January 14, 1957, Director Fritjof Nordborg composed a memorandum, intentionally avoiding legalese, to indicate what the complicated terminology actually signified. He wrote:

To keep it simple, let's say *Andrea Doria* was worth $28 million, the repairs to *Stockholm* cost $1 million, and third-party claims amount to $6 million, for a total of $35 million. This means Swedish America Line's contribution, approximately $4.5 million, amounts to approximately 13 percent of the total, which means Italian Line's share is 87 percent. As far as Swedish America Line is concerned, of course, as was obvious in the insurance arrangements, everything is taken care of except the loss of business and certain costs not covered in the insurance policy.

However, under the terms of the agreement with the underwriters in London, Swedish America Line has been granted compensation for these otherwise uninsured damages by a sum not to exceed $200,000. The bottom line is that loss of business is the only item for which Swedish America Line is not compensated.

Under the settlement, the big loser was *Andrea Doria*'s owner, Italian Line. The real value of *Andrea Doria* was estimated at between $28 and $35 million, but the insurers paid out only $16 million. Even Swedish America Line rightly pointed out that this sum did not correspond to the ship's true worth.

Italian sources maintained vigorously that *Andrea Doria* was underinsured. The newspaper *Italian Line Borghese* published an article on August 10, 1956, that included the following observation:

The accident included one thing to be reckoned with, something that has been hidden from the public. *Andrea Doria* cost 16 billion lire to construct, yet the ship was insured for only some 10 billion lire.

At the time of the accident, one dollar was equivalent to 5.18 Swedish krona, and a billion lire was worth 8.3 million Swedish krona. The newspaper article continued:

Some newspapers have tried to make their readers believe the low insurance took into account four years' "wear and tear" of the ship. Engineers, state officials, and managers of Finmare have said *Andrea Doria* was not insured against total loss because she was "unsinkable." Idiots may swallow that argument, but the Italian people deserve better than to have such nonsense spread out for their consumption.

And just for the record, a floating vessel cannot be "unsinkable." No private shipowner sends its ships—not even the most modern of them—to sea without total insurance coverage. Talking about wear and tear is totally beside the point because today's ships are extremely well built.

CHAPTER 17

Battle over Blame

All of the parties involved in the collision between *Stockholm* and *Andrea Doria* could finally stop worrying on January 24, 1957. A binding settlement had been reached between Swedish America Line and Italian Line and had been certified by Judge Walsh.

There was a common desire to have as little as possible written and discussed about the accident which had captured the world's attention for so many months. The theoretical possibility of a trial still existed, but no one deemed it likely.

The aim was that the agreement would not be made public in its entirety. Though previously the media had broadcast every syllable uttered during the preliminary hearing, the details of the settlement were shrouded in fog.

By January 24, not only had both parties officially agreed, but they had also patiently and circumspectly worked out, word by prudent word, the following communique for simultaneous release in Sweden and the United States:

The boards of Italian Line and Swedish America Line have examined and approved the terms of agreement recently proposed in London by representatives of both companies with the participation of the insurance underwriters.

This agreement does not address misconduct or responsibility; its primary purpose is to facilitate and expedite the lawful claims of third parties, and both companies have instructed their attorneys in New York to cooperate in settling such claims as quickly as possible.

This was a very labored communique of two long sentences, authored by legal experts for both parties and carefully examined by the executive officers of both companies. No opportunity was given the companies' public relations departments to influence the wording in an attempt to clarify the settlement—that was not the intention.

However, the drama was soon to change. It would be no exaggeration to say Swedish America Line's management and its legal experts were "fit to be tied" the following day when a spokesman for the Italian company released a statement about the compensation issue that was not in accord with the facts. It was quoted by the news agency, the *United Press International*. The spokesman was alleged to have said in an interview that Lloyd's of London would probably have to pay the Italian Line nine-tenths of the damages suffered by the company through the loss of *Andrea Doria* and Swedish America Line would receive compensation for one-tenth of the damages to *Stockholm.*

Swedish America Line regarded these assertions as a provocation by the Italians. From the strictly financial point of view, after all, the London agreement had suggested *Andrea Doria* was about 90 percent at fault. Now the Italians had come out with an assertion that turned everything upside down and indirectly insinuated that Swedish America Line had admitted *it* was 90 percent to blame.

The Italian spokesman's gambit might possibly have been intended for domestic consumption. However, little by little the Italian public had begun to realize the navigation of *Andrea Doria* in the fog off Nantucket had not been managed with the required competence. The public had also had difficulty understanding how a ship that was supposed to be "unsinkable" had in fact gone down so quickly. Critical voices in the Italian media were becoming more strident. It might have been deemed opportune for Italian Line to construct a suitable closing scene in which *Andrea Doria* was portrayed as almost entirely without fault for the collision.

Swedish America Line reacted instantly to this new situation, and both the Swedish and the international press were sent the following communique:

> The statements issued by a spokesman for Italian Line do not conform to the facts. Swedish America Line finds it difficult to understand that representatives of Italian Line could present this kind of statement in contravention of what they know to be the truth. Swedish America Line has contacted Italian Line in Genoa and requested an immediate explanation, inasmuch as the two companies

had agreed that neither party should for the present make any comments about the London agreement over and above the joint communique already published.

Swedish America Line went on to point out that the possibility of a trial in New York had not been written off. This reminder was to be interpreted as an indirect threat to annul the London agreement and move on to regular court proceedings unless the Italian Line issued a disclaimer.

To put further pressure on the Italians, the cable went on to say Swedish America Line and the Association of Swedish Steamship Underwriters regarded themselves as immediately free to publish correct and detailed information about the negotiations in New York unless they received a satisfactory reply.

Italian Line responded immediately in a communique sent out by the Italian news agency ANSA:

> The rumor that a spokesman for Italian Line might have violated the London agreement by disclosing details included in it to the press is completely unfounded. Italian Line has only submitted to the press a communique that an agreement has been reached by both companies. That communique has been worked out in cooperation with Swedish America Line.

At this point, Swedish America Line and the Underwriters Association decided to put their threat into action and publicize all the details of the London agreement. What had happened was without doubt a welcome opportunity for Swedish America Line's administrators in both Gothenburg and New York to absolve themselves from the accusations of responsibility they knew the Italians were spreading to the mass media off the record.

Now the companies could end their discussions regarding fault. Instead, they began to handle third-party claims as expeditiously as possible in order to reach common accord with everyone involved.

According to Swedish law, maritime hearings regarding a collision should be held before the Swedish Consul General in New York or in a Swedish court. It did not seem necessary to hold these hearings, however, since the detailed testimony given in New York provided a good picture of what had occurred before, during, and after the collision off Nantucket. The investigation conducted by the Swedish Board of Shipping and Navigation called particular attention to the prevailing weather conditions as the most important factor contributing to the collision.

Andrea Doria had proceeded in heavy fog from 1500 until the time *Stockholm* was sighted. The Swedish ship had enjoyed relatively good visibility almost the entire time from her departure from New York up to the last minute before the collision.

Hence, according to the judgment of the Swedish Board of Shipping and Navigation, the collision must have occurred at the edge of a fogbank from which one ship, *Andrea Doria,* loomed suddenly and toward which the other ship, *Stockholm,* was heading. The board's technical adviser summed it up as follows:

Andrea Doria's maneuver to turn to port before *Stockholm* was actually sighted, combined with the visibility conditions and the high speed of both ships, are the major reasons for the collision. There appear to be no accusations to be made, with the visibility conditions verified, concerning the mate's decision to alter course as executed by *Stockholm.* This applies no matter whether the decision was made to avoid a collision or to ensure a safe passing distance between the ships.

In all substantial respects, the report cleared *Stockholm a*nd the mate in charge of responsibility for the accident.

The discussion of what "moderate speed" might have meant under the prevailing weather conditions ended in the observation that *Stockholm,* according to tests carried out, could reduce her speed from full ahead to dead in the water in 350 meters. Since this distance was appreciably less than the visible distance at the time, her speed had been deemed justifiable.

Based on the report of the technical consultant, the maritime prosecutor's decision was as follows:

Having studied the results of the investigation concerning the collision between the motor vessels *Stockholm* and *Andrea Doria,* as well as the memorandum from the maritime engineering consultant, I conclude there are no circumstances requiring a pretrial inquiry.

As far as the Swedish interests were concerned, that decision, dated October 19, 1957, concluded the *Stockholm–Andrea Doria* case.

It took four years from the time of the collision before all damage claims were processed. The claims finally approved and paid out had by then been reduced to 5.9 million Swedish krona. This left $600,000 in *Stockholm'*s so-called "limitation of liability" fund. In accordance with the settlement, this amount was turned over to *Andrea Doria*'s underwriters.

But what happened in Italy? By and large, there was a deafening silence, even if one or another journalist demanded to hear all the facts. It was known that the Minister for Maritime Affairs had appointed a commission of inquiry at an early stage, and the commission had not been able to agree on a statement because it might "stain the glory of Italian shipping."

As late as 1973, the respected Italian newspaper *Corriera Della Sera,* which had conducted its own extensive investigation, published the following:

We have been in contact with various persons who are in a position to know the circumstances surrounding the event, but we have come up empty-handed. The shipping company, Italian Line, says that it will not comment on the affair out of consideration for the commission of inquiry. We don't know whether that commission has reached any conclusion, but in any case, they have not released one. Perhaps it is carefully stored in some safe.

Even today, no official final report has been made. Yet, one result is irrefutable: the tragic loss of *Andrea Doria,* the pride of the Italian merchant fleet, cast a gloomy shadow over Italian trade and shipping, over *Andrea Doria*'s owner Italian Line, and over her builders, the Ansaldo Shipyard, for many years to come.

CHAPTER 18

The New *Gripsholm* Arrives from Ansaldo

As noted earlier, *Stockholm* was an unwanted child, a bad luck ship for the people in Sweden and America who tried to market her services. The greatest disappointment was registered in the United States, where Swedish America Line's prewar ships, the White Viking Fleet, had previously been marketed as floating hotels, floating palaces, and the beauties of the seas.

These various appellations, written by clever marketing people, created expectations of luxury and comfort combined with peace and quiet during the crossing. *Stockholm* could meet the demands for good service in every respect, but not much more.

Eventually, even Swedish America Line's management realized its decision to build an "economy ship" was wrong. The company had erroneously estimated the market—particularly in the United States.

As an admission of its own mistake, the company decided to build a larger, "proper" Swedish America ship a couple of years after *Stockholm* had been delivered. The new ship, called *Kungsholm,* arrived in 1953 from the Schelde Shipyard in Vlissingen, the Neth-

erlands. The order of a new *Gripsholm* in 1954 confirmed that Swedish America Line had reverted to its earlier policy and would have two fine ships equally suitable for cruising or transatlantic crossings.

In conjunction with ordering *Gripsholm,* Swedish America Line tried to dispose of *Stockholm,* either totally or partially. Although the ship had been reconstructed to provide larger passenger capacity and a movie theater on the forecastle, she still did not measure up to expectations, in particular for the American market.

The dream of an "SAS at Sea" had sometimes crossed the minds of Swedish America Line's management. In early 1955 Erik Wijk turned to the three dominant Danish passenger line companies and offered them an agreement by which *Stockholm* would be registered as a Danish ship.

The reply came quickly. The three Danish passenger line companies unanimously rejected the Swedish offer and added: "Incidentally, we do not regard Swedish America Line's *Stockholm* as suitable for such service." This judgment caused considerable irritation for Swedish America Line, which regarded Denmark as an important component in Scandinavian transport operations.

Still, Swedish America Line was reluctant to give up the idea of placing *Stockholm* on the Danish market, and hence arranged for a Danish America Line to be formed by people in Copenhagen who had connections with the Swedish company. *Stockholm* would be furnished with Danish furniture, and the office in Copenhagen would be expanded at great cost. Yet, despite all this, the project was not successful.

Stockholm was a ship that nobody really wanted, and the management of Swedish America Line was relieved when East Germany offered to buy her in 1960. She was rechristened *Völkerfreundschaft* and, under the management of Stena Lines, she made many cruises originating in Gothenburg.

As for *Gripsholm*, according to plan, the Ansaldo Shipyard in Genoa should have delivered her at the end of 1956, but for various reasons, there was a delay of about half a year. Due to her size, the new *Gripsholm* would become the premier ship not only of Swedish America Line, but also of the entire Swedish merchant fleet.

The question of who was to command the new Swedish America ship was an ongoing matter of discussion both inside and outside Swedish America Line. The two obvious candidates for the post were John Nordlander, captain of *Kungsholm*, and Gunnar Nordenson, captain of the unlucky *Stockholm*.

Which one would be awarded the coveted position?

John Nordlander, captain of Swedish America Line's biggest ship at the time, *Kungsholm*, thought it was perfectly evident that he should assume command of the newer and bigger *Gripsholm*.

Gunnar Nordenson, totally occupied with defending himself and his ship in the New York court, could not, or more accurately would not, involve himself in this battle over careers.

Yet, Captain Nordlander was all the more determined to realize his wish and sent an ultimatum to the president of Swedish America Line, Erik Wijk: "If I am not appointed captain of the new *Gripsholm,* I will resign!" said Nordlander. Wijk accepted the resignation.

In a final attempt to obtain the desired appointment as captain of *Gripsholm,* Captain Nordlander turned to Ann-Ida Broström, but she explained that she neither would nor could involve herself in the appointment and told Captain Nordlander to accept that. Hearing that response, the captain turned to Wijk and asked to withdraw his resignation but that was not done. That was why one of Swedish America Line's most experienced captains had to look elsewhere for employment.

Now the company was free to appoint Gunnar Nordenson as captain of the new *Gripsholm,* which pleased Swedish America Line's management for two reasons:

1. As captain of their biggest ship, they had acquired a person who was most willing to cooperate.

2. They had been able to demonstrate to the whole world that Captain Nordenson enjoyed the full confidence of his company despite the terrible collision in which his prior ship had been involved.

However, the appointment of Captain Nordenson was not made public until the joint agreement between Italian Line and Swedish America Line had been finalized, due to fear of complications or additional delays regarding the delivery of *Gripsholm* from the Ansaldo shipbuilders.

It did not seem appropriate for Captain Nordenson to journey down to the Ansaldo yard to follow the action as work on *Gripsholm* was being completed. Hence, the captain got his first look at the ship he was to command from the reviewing stand on Swedish America Line's pier in Gothenburg.

Carstens was appointed senior third mate on *Gripsholm*. Along with the other officers, he was to go to the Ansaldo yard to acquaint himself with the ship and sail on her as she made the journey to Gothenburg. Carstens had his ticket and was at the station waiting for departure when someone from the personnel section stopped him. At the very last minute, someone realized that it might not be such a good idea to send him to the Ansaldo yard in Genoa. After all, it had not been very long ago that Italian Line and Swedish America Line had reached their agreement about the collision between *Stockholm* and *Andrea Doria*, and there was little doubt that bitter feelings about the crew of the Swedish ship remained in Italy.

If the one person who, according to the Italians, was chiefly responsible for the loss of *Andrea Doria* should suddenly appear at the shipyard, it might cause complications: harassment of Carstens and maybe even a work shutdown on *Gripsholm*. She was already overdue by several months, and there must not be further delay. Therefore, Carstens and Captain Nordenson awaited the arrival of *Gripsholm* in Gothenburg.

Gripsholm's arrival had been carefully planned, down to the day and the hour. It was always a major event when a newly built passenger ship arrived in Gothenburg from abroad, and *Gripsholm* was in no way to be an exception!

All signs indicated that the traditional kind of passenger traffic across the Atlantic was dwindling to the point of disappearance. Perhaps *Gripsholm* would be the last of her kind. On April 22, 1957, she was scheduled to arrive at Gothenburg, and she did so, at about lunchtime.

At least a hundred thousand citizens of Gothenburg and others from western Sweden turned up: the arrival of a new "America boat" was not to be missed. Gothenburg's harbor was still in most respects open, where people could move about freely.

This freedom was realized not only on the occasion of the arrival or departure of an "America boat," but also on holidays and weekends, when a promenade in the harbor area was among the most popular activities.

The entry of *Gripsholm* into the harbor in Gothenburg was thus magnificent. Minesweepers from the Western Naval Command had already greeted her at the limit of territorial waters, and later, a number of other naval ships and ten tugboats from the Red Company (owned by the Broströms) joined in the welcoming flotilla. The navy's Honor Guard was positioned at the entrance to the harbor, and once inside the harbor, *Gripsholm* received an escort of fireboats which heralded her final approach to the pier with their water "fireworks." In line with tradition, when a new "America boat" arrived, the sirens of all the ships currently on hand greeted her.

Per Nyström, the county governor, welcomed *Gripsholm* to her home port, and Erik Wijk replied to the governor's speech from the ship's bridge. The *Nidinge* lightship foghorn—the oldest in the world, now located in the Maritime Museum—sounded, and the navy orchestra played from the roof of Swedish America Line's pier. A new era had begun, not only for Swedish America Line but also for Broströms, at that time one of the foremost shipowners in the world.

A good number of the Broström dynasty had gathered, led by Ann-Ida. For Captain Gunnar Nordenson, it was a great moment when he and Carstens could go on board and take command of the ship, which, in his case, would be his last command.

Gripsholm's maiden voyage to New York would be by way of Copenhagen, which was an important link for Swedish America Line in its transatlantic service. It was very important to show off the new acquisition for the media, the tourist agencies, and the authorities in the capital city of Denmark.

Unlike Captain Calamai of *Andrea Doria*, Captain Nordenson had been entrusted with a new ship. Not only that, it was the principal ship of the Swedish merchant fleet. It was also important for Carstens to have been appointed to the *Gripsholm*, proving that he had the unquestioned confidence of his company. It was a testimony to his conduct on the bridge on that fateful night when he encountered *Andrea Doria* off Nantucket and also during the preliminary hearing in New York.

If *Gripsholm*'s arrival in Gothenburg and the call at Copenhagen were grand occasions, her entrance into New York harbor was practically triumphant. It began with a rendezvous off the coast of North America with the old *Gripsholm*, which had been delivered to Swedish America Line in 1925 and had been rechristened *Berlin* under the German flag. Cables were exchanged.

At the quarantine station, the American frigate *Laring* saluted *Gripsholm*, and then she was followed up the Hudson River by a swarm of tugboats, fireboats, and pleasure boats of every kind. Airplanes and helicopters buzzed in the skies, and ships anchored in the harbor sounded their horns as she passed various docks and piers.

During the last few years, Swedish America Line had garnered a great deal of attention thanks to the collision between its *Stockholm* and *Andrea Doria*. It was perfectly obvious the collision and the preliminary hearing had *not* damaged Swedish America Line's reputation—quite the contrary. Now that the Swedish company was able to present a new ship, interest was at its highest point, and the positive judgments about the new *Gripsholm* were conspicuous. This attention was evident not only from the usual newspapers that were interested in good Swedish-American relations, but also from the purely American press, led by the *New York Times*.

As *Gripsholm* went into service, the next-to-the-last page in the history of Swedish America Line had been turned. One more ship, *Kungsholm*, would bring an end to what had been perhaps the proudest era in Swedish maritime history.

CHAPTER 19

Andrea Doria v. *Stockholm:*
An Imagined Conversation

The preliminary hearing in New York had been very difficult and trying for both parties. What would have happened had there been a formal court trial with everything at stake—maritime honor, money and market share, and a possible judgment?

Outwardly, it appeared the differences between the two main parties were insurmountable. The two principal protagonists, the attorneys Charles Haight and Eugene Underwood, almost seemed to be mortal enemies as they defended the interests of their clients. The sixty-three-year-old Underwood played on every string available to him. Younger by ten years, Haight maintained his calm temperament and coolness throughout all phases of the hearing. If one could say that two entirely different ships had collided off Nantucket, it could also be said that two entirely different attorneys collided in the courtroom.

This courtroom conduct did not imply, however, that the two men were on bad terms otherwise. The attorneys for Italian Line and Swedish America Line occasionally shared informal conversations and get-togethers. Then, they were colleagues, but in court they remained vigorous opponents. Though Underwood was occasionally tough during the hearing, he was capable of showing appreciation for his adversaries. For example, Carstens remembered with pleasure the first and only time he met the feared attorney outside the courtroom. This meeting occurred after the hearing in, of all places, the men's room. The two men had a friendly exchange, during which Underwood professed his regard for the young mate.

A trial about *Andrea Doria* would have been the maritime law case of the century. A lot of people still are deeply disappointed that it never happened. First and foremost, members of the legal profession would have comprised an enormous throng— judges, attorneys, and experts on maritime law and ship stability. Many others would be involved. Public relations people, for instance, would represent the different parties, and they were predicted to play a major role when it came to influencing public opinion about what was to happen.

Interest in having a proper trial was not limited to the actors on stage or in the wings, but extended also to those who made a living from catastrophes and major accidents.

That segment of the general public that was interested in maritime matters, a larger group than one might think, also had its expectations, not just for heartrending testimony replete with thrusts and parries and pleas in an unusually publicized drama, but also for a final decision.

As things developed, the combatants had entered the ring and fought their preliminary rounds, but no decision had been handed down. It had been an exhibition match in which the combatants sometimes threw punches in the air and sometimes pulled their punches so as not to reveal their techniques and strengths.

What surprises might a real trial have offered? Certainly not many where the collision itself was concerned. In that context, all of the essential personnel had been heard, and the record from the preliminary hearing could be simply registered in court and added to the available documents. Yet, the overriding question would surely remain: "Why did *Andrea Doria* sink?"

It is quite natural to speculate about what might have happened in court. No one can know precisely what the outcome would have been, but it is assumed that whatever advantages the steamship companies had accumulated would have been utilized to the breaking point. Today, if the attorneys for the Swedes and the Italians could access all the material and talk about it without prejudice, the result would surely be a most interesting conversation.

Since such a meeting is not possible, it must be imagined. The attorneys for the two vessels would meet at Fraunces Tavern, a popular pub in lower Manhattan, which harked back to the days of George Washington and which was customarily frequented by members of the legal profession during the 1950s. The Swedish representative will have Swedish America Line's top-secret documents in his briefcase; the Italian representative will have the equivalent documents from Italian Line and the Ansaldo Shipyard. These imaginary attorneys can play roles which were never possible for Underwood and Haight during the hearing. So let the imaginary conversation begin!

Andrea Doria's **attorney:** Perhaps you believe that a court of law would have addressed only the stability of *Andrea Doria*. In that case you woefully underestimate my ability to lead a trial into different paths. There were other more important things to discuss, even though you might dismiss them as insignificant.

I would certainly have wanted to question Third Mate Carstens-Johannsen, and especially Captain Nordenson, about whether it was quite in line with company policy that only one officer would be on watch on the bridge.

Since time has gone by, I have scrutinized the records of the preliminary hearing to refresh my memory. According to these records, something like the following question was addressed to Captain Nordenson: "Do you believe it would have been desirable to have two officers on the bridge of *Stockholm*, considering the weather conditions and the heavy traffic at sea?" Nordenson said he did not really know how to reply to this question. He pointed out that he was following orders and always had one qualified mate on watch when the visibility and the weather conditions were satisfactory. "But," he continued, "if Swedish America Line so decides, I have nothing against having two such officers on the bridge."

Andrea Doria's **attorney continues:** That was indeed an interesting reply, and naturally, I wonder how Swedish America Line would have reacted and begun its investigation.

By coincidence, a quite ordinary person thrust a piece of paper into my hand. It was a summary of the hearing with Captain Nordenson, accompanied by commentaries from Swedish America Line. I was amazed. It had to do with a blistering criticism of the captain's pronouncements and reactions. In critical terms, Swedish America Line emphasized they had not stipulated whether there should be one or two officers on the bridge. They further maintained that the commander of *Stockholm* had both the freedom and the option of appointing an extra mate on the bridge "in crowded waters or whenever else he deems it appropriate."

My dear friend, you may be sure that I would have pressed Captain Nordenson to the limit on this point. Of course, one can describe the area around Nantucket (sometimes referred to as the Times Square of the Atlantic) as "crowded waters," so two officers on the bridge of *Stockholm* would have been advisable on this fateful night. And in this response, I overlook the thickening fog.

***Andrea Doria's* attorney continues:** I trust you recall Third Mate Carstens-Johannsen's testimony during the preliminary hearing. How could he have managed everything that had to be done during the minutes prior to the collision—check out a forgetful helmsman, keep a lookout, read the radar, plot the course, and personally see what is happening ahead. To accomplish this would be a job for at least two people. *Andrea Doria* had *three* officers on her bridge.

***Stockholm's* attorney:** If this statement had been made in court, I would have protested loudly. But go on.

***Andrea Doria's* attorney:** Of course, all the work that Carstens-Johannsen did on the bridge was in line with predetermined routines—I'm aware of that. Presumably the course of events leading up to the collision would not have been influenced whether there were one or two mates on the bridge, but I would have pointed out the young and, in my opinion, inexperienced mate as a contrast to all of the qualified officers on *Andrea Doria's* bridge where calm prevailed and everything was checked in detail. That comparison might have made a certain psychological impression on the judge.

***Stockholm's* attorney:** Is that it?

***Andrea Doria's* attorney:** No, certainly not. Naturally we also knew what happened when *Stockholm* returned to New York without her bow. There on the bridge stood the same mate—in the middle of the night—solely responsible for a ship that could sink at any moment.

In this part of the trial, I would have really challenged Captain Nordenson's conduct, and I would have made certain comparisons. Assigning a lone mate on *Stockholm's* bridge in a heavily trafficked fairway with the risk of fog showed the same poor judgment by the captain as putting the same mate alone on the bridge with sole responsibility for a badly damaged ship on the approach to New York.

***Stockholm's* attorney:** What you are saying now might possibly have been your best argument. As an experienced expert in maritime law, how do you think the judge might have reacted?

***Andrea Doria's* attorney:** In an American court, the one who weighs the facts (in admiralty cases, that is the judge, not a jury) can always be swayed, especially if a presentation were spiced with feelings of sentimentality, a deep concern for all the people involved.

***Stockholm's* attorney:** In no way do I doubt your thespian talents, but what does this really have to do with the collision and the sinking of *Andrea Doria*?

***Andrea Doria's* attorney:** Actually, nothing at all, but it would have put you on the defensive. I would also have raised another issue which had previously been neglected:

```
m/v STOCKHOLM - s/s ANDREA DORIA

Additional points developed in telephone discussion
     of Mr. Haight with Mr. J. L. Wilson,
  supplementing Mr. Wilson's letter to Mr. Haight
              dated September 4, 1956.

        The Stockholm photographs show more damage on

the port bow, and Wilson's opinion is that the damage

shows that the angle of collision was about 30 to 45

degrees between the starboard side of the Doria and the

port side of the Stockholm (i.e., the angle leading aft).
```

Note from maritime engineer J. Lyell Wilson to Charles Haight regarding collision angle.

Stockholm's stability or, more properly speaking, her erratic behavior at sea. I would have requested all of her logbooks, purser's reports, and so on.

Then, with great feeling, I would have read aloud reports of what had happened on board ever since 1948: about *Stockholm*'s unpredictable movements even in quite calm weather; about passengers who had been injured and died; about furniture that had been knocked around; about glass and china that had been smashed; about the failed attempt that had been made to stabilize her by ballasting her with 3,000 tons of stone.

Andrea Doria's **attorney continues:** Can you stand to hear how I would have gone about orchestrating the summing up of my case? I would have said something like this: "Your Honor, the assassin of *Andrea Doria* was a ship dogged by bad luck from the start, a ship with questionable, albeit lawful, stability. You have heard the story of a second-rate ship called into question by her

owners even before she was built, unsteady and haunted by accidents throughout her voyages thus far. Unluckily enough, she found herself in the difficult situation of being navigated by an inexperienced officer while her captain rested in his cabin.

"Sailing back to New York after the collision and the sinking of *Andrea Doria,* the same mate was put in charge on the bridge while the captain went below to sleep.

"Your Honor, I dare to assert that to be young and inexperienced is one thing, to be old and injudicious is another. But when these two conditions are combined, they create a serious problem—indeed, it borders on criminality!"

Stockholm's **attorney:** I would have to object strongly. I may have put up with a great deal, but this assertion goes too far.

Andrea Doria's **attorney:** Forgive my choice of words; the observation was perhaps somewhat exaggerated. But my only chance was to pursue the path established in the preliminary hearing: hammer into the judge that Mate Carstens-Johannsen was young and inexperienced and that Captain Nordenson was injudicious when he assigned him to the bridge yet one more time.

Weren't you worried that I might exploit that?

Stockholm's **attorney:** Yes, of course I was, but Captain Nordenson had firmly stated that putting Carstens-Johannsen back in charge on the bridge was an affirmation of the degree to which he trusted him. He also wanted to bolster his self-esteem. Obviously, we had to trust Captain Nordenson in all situations, considering how matters developed.

Andrea Doria's **attorney:** All right, let's leave it at that. As I said, I'm not sure that affects the point at issue, but you can at least admit that it would really have shaken you up. And by the way, what surprises did your side have to present?

Stockholm's **attorney:** Nothing in particular with regard to the collision and Carstens-Johannsen's prior maneuvers. The other people on the bridge—the helmsman and the lookout—had been heard and had given unequivocal testimony in Carstens's favor. Naturally, we would have introduced the different photos of *Stockholm's* bow, pictures that proved the collision angle was between 30° and 45°.

That fact supports Carstens's reading of *Andrea Doria's* erratic maneuvers.

Captain Nordenson had indeed seen nothing, but he gave his moral support. The telegraph operators and machinists had also testified. As far as we were concerned, there was nothing essential to be added. I think everyone behaved well, even exceptionally well. Carstens-Johannsen was quite simply brilliant as he was questioned day after day. If this whole thing had in fact gone to trial, we would not have needed to question our own people again. But there were others.

Andrea Doria's **attorney:** The principal witnesses?

Stockholm's **attorney:** Well, you can call them that if you will. As you are surely aware, almost the whole time during the construction of *Andrea Doria*, there was a ferocious battle between her owners, Italian Line, and her builders, the Ansaldo Shipyard.

The main and overriding issue was stability—what should and should not be done to fulfill all the regulations. There was enormous disagreement and the issues often boiled down to personal animosities between representatives of the steamship company and of the shipyard.

We learned about all this at a very early stage. After all, we had very good connections with the shipyard, since Swedish America Line was in the process of building the new *Gripsholm* there. You, if anyone, ought to know how to keep informed and plug leaks.

Andrea Doria's **attorney:** If you had said in court what you have just said here, I would of course have objected vehemently. Now, in retrospect, I admit the stability calculations for the Italian Line that were submitted to the court in New York at the conclusion of the hearing came as somewhat of a shock. It was then that we realized the end might be near, but we still had to keep up appearances.

Stockholm's **attorney:** I felt sorry for Captain Calamai right from the start. He knew that in terms of stability, *Andrea Doria* was not well built, but he and Italian Line hoped this would never be revealed. It was not only the fact that Captain Calamai had lost his ship through unfortunate circumstances, but he had also landed in an indefensible position.

Naturally, I would have been forced to request the logbooks. For me, it would have probably been necessary to summon Captain Calamai as a witness once again and to press him yet once more about the construction of *Andrea Doria* when he sailed out with her on her maiden voyage.

Yet, the question remains: do I not suffer just as much as you and Italian Line do now when the issues of stability calculations are to be presented to the court? In line with the Bonner Committee report previously introduced, this seems to be pouring salt into open wounds.

***Andrea Doria*'s attorney:** Let's leave that. We were speaking earlier about "principal witnesses." Who might they be?

***Stockholm*'s attorney:** For obvious reasons, I cannot name names, but I can offer you some enlightenment to steer you in the direction of an educated guess.

The minister of the Italian merchant fleet appointed a commission immediately after the collision. Its task was to try to figure out how the accident could have happened and why *Andrea Doria* went down. As the inquiry proceeded, the stability issue became predominant, and all kinds of calculations were made, including those made by using a 14-meter-long model of the ship constructed just for that purpose.

Everybody agreed *Andrea Doria*'s stability was poor, especially toward the end of any voyage. But who was responsible? From the start, Italian Line pointed the finger at the Ansaldo Shipyard and its technicians, accusing them of making defective calculations and producing slipshod construction.

As time went by the antagonism grew, until finally the Ansaldo Shipyard was concerned that the accusations were putting its entire reputation at stake.

I have here a copy of a document Swedish America Line obtained from "absolutely reliable sources" in Italy. The document made a number of detours before reaching the Swedish Embassy in Rome, which in turn forwarded it to the Swedish State Department in Stockholm.

The message had been stamped "confidential," but Swedish America Line received a copy immediately. I am sure you realize that this was not a matter of gossip. The Ansaldo Shipyard was really fighting for its reputation and its survival.

Even though *Stockholm*'s owners were already aware of a number of things that appeared in the document, the paper itself provided valuable confirmation. For example, I can mention Swedish America Line's technicians noted in a memorandum dated as early as December 12, 1956, that calculations dealing with *Andrea Doria* had not been signed and had not been approved by any authority.

I presume that you can figure out where this document originated on the basis of what I have said, and also what principal witnesses we would have called if there had been a trial.

***Andrea Doria*'s attorney:** I can draw my conclusions, but I doubt those witnesses would really have stood up and testified. As you know, Italians are very jealous of their honor when it comes to shipping and navigation, and the content of this document, had it been confirmed by witnesses in a trial, would really have defiled that honor.

***Stockholm*'s attorney:** I think we can agree that the preliminary hearing changed character toward the end. The collision itself somehow acquired a minor role; interest shifted instead to the question of why *Andrea Doria* sank—and more specifically why she went to the bottom the *way* she did.

***Andrea Doria*'s attorney:** I know you have mentioned this matter before. You mean that she did not go down bow first or stern first, but sank straight down?

***Stockholm*'s attorney:** Exactly. Carstens-Johannsen said at one point *Andrea Doria* went down like a whale, and I think that simile was quite significant. As you know, all of us on both sides tried to secure all kinds of evidence that might be usable in a coming

Shortly after the sinking of *Andrea Doria,* the Swedish America Line received stability computations from *Gripsholm* which was being built in the yard which had built *Andrea Doria*—the Ansaldo yard in Genoa. The calculations were made by technical experts, and Swedish America Line's chief attorney in Gothenburg stated in a strictly confidential memo to Charles S. Haight that if this was the usual way to establish a ship's stability in Italy, *Andrea Doria* may not have been "satisfactorily constructed" from a stability point of view.

trial. And to be quite honest, I have to admit Italian Line was obliging, even if you were sometimes uncooperative, for understandable reasons.

You often went on board *Stockholm* and conducted inspections both on the bridge and in other locations after a witness had testified. I can understand that you wanted to make sure that everything checked out.

I particularly recall one occasion when you pressured Carstens-Johannsen about a certain statement of time. He had said that from his position by the radar apparatus he could see the ship's clock in the wheelhouse. In no time at all, you were up on *Stockholm* at the Bethlehem Steel Shipyard, checking this information.

Andrea Doria's attorney: Yes, we spared no effort to catch any errors on his part. He was, after all, the main witness, and every possible inaccuracy in his testimony, however insignificant it might appear to be, naturally had to be used.

Stockholm's attorney: Of course, you had obvious advantages when you made your inspections. *Stockholm* was right there in New York, whereas *Andrea Doria* lay at a depth of 70 meters off Nantucket. As luck would have it, *Andrea Doria*'s sister ship, *Cristoforo Colombo,* arrived in New York a short while after the collision. Then we had our technicians go on board and check out what were for us very significant details concerning her construction.

Andrea Doria's attorney: In principle, everything was accessible for inspection, and since *Cristoforo Colombo* was an exact copy of *Andrea Doria* in terms of construction, we could not object to your investigations on board her. If we had refused, you would of course have turned to the court and maintained that we had something to hide, and your public relations people would naturally have made use of that.

But I can assure you there was plenty of excitement when you returned with photographers and big floodlights.

Stockholm's **attorney:** As you know, it's far from easy to get good photos of such huge areas as the engine room and generator room on a big ship. They would have to be as clear as possible. We did not want only overall views, we wanted details. The details were most interesting, and they were what we wanted to document before anything happened.

Andrea Doria's **attorney:** What do you mean, "happened?" We obviously could not rebuild a huge engine room, or sink *Cristoforo Colombo* in New York Harbor!

Stockholm's **attorney:** No, of course not. I can assure you we never actually entertained thoughts of such a conspiracy. On the other hand, it would be a simple matter to put in doors where none existed before. And that is why we went on board *Cristoforo Colombo* as soon as we could. We inspected her and took a lot of photographs.

Andrea Doria's **attorney:** And what did you find?

Stockholm's **attorney:** Nothing that appeared remarkable at first glance. But we had previously studied the blueprints of *Andrea Doria* with regard to the engine room, the generator room, tanks, and watertight bulkheads, and we had made a number of interesting observations. Among other things, we discovered there was a tunnel running all the way from the bow to the generator room.

It seemed there was no door between the tunnel and the neighboring area, and that was confirmed when we went below on

Cristoforo Colombo. We photographed the area to secure evidence.

Andrea Doria's **attorney:** The existence of a tunnel or passageway in the bow can have no connection with the sinking of *Andrea Doria,* even if there were no doors to other areas.

Stockholm's **attorney:** On the contrary, the tunnel might have been a factor in the sinking. Farthest down in the hull, the hole that resulted from the collision was small. What happened was the lower section of *Stockholm's* bow hit the bottom of *Andrea Doria* right between two oil tanks that were separated by a cofferdam—an empty space that acts as a kind of "security valve" in case one oil tank should begin to leak.

That explains why it was possible for the sea to rush in and fill *Andrea Doria* from the bottom, which is why she sank as she did, filled with water from bow to stern.

Andrea Doria's **attorney:** You've spoken of a "bulls-eye" impact on *Andrea Doria.* If your description is accurate, she was hit at her absolutely most fragile point.

Stockholm's **attorney:** Precisely! The way *Andrea Doria* was constructed, the tunnel was her Achilles heel. But there were other vulnerable places as well. There is a lot to be found in the memorandum I referred to earlier. It stated that the conditions for *Andrea Doria* <u>not</u> sinking after a collision were that "the ship be struck only at the very end of her stem, and at a very narrow entrance angle."

Andrea Doria's **attorney:** Why did you not introduce this at the preliminary hearing? You had photographic evidence and perhaps blueprints as well.

Stockholm's **attorney:** The hearing had not run its course when it was broken off, and if there had not been a settlement between Italian Line and Swedish America Line, *Andrea Doria's* engineers were due to testify. They were very familiar with what had happened in their domain.

```
                                    September 24, 1957  Wk/im

Mr. Charles S. Haight
Haight, Gardner, Poor & Havens
80 Broad Street
New York 4, N.Y.

Private and confidential

Dear Charlie:

From an Italian source which is considered more reliable than most I
received the other day some rather interesting information in
connection with the ANDREA DORIA. The report was handed to me
translated from Italian into Swedish and we have now made a
translation of the Swedish version into English, which you will find
enclosed. The language is not too good, but it is partly explained by
the fact that it is a translation of a translation. Anyhow I believe
that you might get some valuable information out of the report. I take
it that nothing should be done at the present time in regard to the
collision as such, but at a later date when the case has been settled
in New York, this information might be of use.

                               With kindest regards
                               Sincerely yours




bcc: Direktör Fritjof Nordborg
Enc.
```

Cover letter to Charles S. Haight, which accompanied a confidential memorandum received by the Swedish Embassy in Rome.

Personally, I regret that it was not possible to interrogate them. Their responses would have been interesting, very interesting! Besides, the engineers were irritated with Captain Calamai for implying that it was a problem in the steering system that caused *Andrea Doria's* final, inexplicable maneuver.

Yet, I am not sure Swedish America Line would have introduced its pictures and blueprints at the hearing even then. The matter might have proceeded to a full trial, and in that case it wouldn't have hurt to keep some evidence in reserve.

Andrea Doria's **attorney:** Do you really believe Swedish America Line would have won if there had been a trial?

Stockholm's **attorney:** Believe? I am certain! Who do you think would have won?

Andrea Doria's **attorney:** During all my years in American courtrooms I have learned one thing—anything can happen.

Yet, whether Italian Line would have won this particular case—I doubt it.

Very shortly after the sinking of *Andrea Doria*, it became clear to the Swedish America Line that the stability of *Andrea Doria* under certain circumstances was not up to par. The Ansaldo shipyard, which had built *Andrea Doria,* had continuously been engaged in arguments with Italian Line officials and technicians. The plans and calculations for the vessel were imperfect and some were not signed. The Italian Line knew about it from absolutely reliable sources, but nevertheless it was not welcome information despite being sprinkled with intricate details. The Italian government authorities had not performed their supervisory function in a proper way.

The following document from the foreign department had been received by the Swedish America Line about eight months after settlement had been reached in New York. If the preliminary hearings had been followed by a court proceeding, the document would have been of extraordinary importance. The Swedish ambassador in Rome had originally obtained the document from the consulate in Naples, but everything indicated that the source was the Ansaldo shipyard in Genoa.

The foreign department in a later letter dealt with how the company was to handle this: the letter should be sent to Swedish America Line's lawyers in New York, but it should not be revealed that the letter came from the Swedish foreign department. Obviously, one should not endanger diplomatic relations.

President Wijk forwarded the document to New York lawyer Haight with information that it came from a reliable Italian source. Wijk assumed that nothing should be done then but that the information could be available at a later time. That time has now come as can be seen from the following confidential letter.

ROYAL
SWEDISH EMBASSY

Encl. with letter by hand,
König-Leijon 5 Sept. '57

Confidential

TRANSLATION

Strictly confidential communication from an absolutely safe source

1.   The vessel *Andrea Doria* had serious design defects. The drawings and design plans were made up very carelessly by inexperienced technicians at the Italia shipyards and approved no less carelessly without checking by the engineers in the Italian Shipping Registry (Registro Italiano Navale, R.I.N.) and by corrupt officials in the Ministry of Merchant Marine.

2.   The Ansaldo yard in Genoa, before beginning to build the vessel, urgently pointed out the serious shortcomings and errors affecting the calculations, but on their own initiative were able only to make some rather important changes to avoid a scandal without hurting the feelings of:

> (a) Mr. Selvino Sornesi, general manager of the
> Italia shipyards, and his technicians, who had
> drawn up the plans for the vessel;
>
> (b) Mr. Barone, admiral in the reserve, chairman
> of the Italian Shipping Registry;
>
> (c) The Ministry of Merchant Marine.

3.   During ongoing construction of the vessel, the shipping registry, according to law, should have inspected operations for subsequent determination of class. Instead, there was no inspection, but all the same when the vessel was launched, it was classified in the "Star Class" (absolute top rating).

4.   The two principal design defects of the *Andrea Doria* were:

> (a) The vessel, with a scant 19-degree list, due
> to external causes, was unable to right itself and
> resume its ordinary equilibrium position.
>
> (b) The conditions for the safety devices to go
> into action quickly in event of a collision were
> that the vessel should be struck only at the
> extreme stem at a very small entrance angle (only
> a few degrees).

5.   Captain Calamai and his officers were not familiar with the use of radar.

6.   When the collision with the *Stockholm* occurred, the *Andrea Doria* was caused to list to starboard by just the aforesaid 19 degrees.

There was not even the slightest attempt to make use of the equilibrium tanks because of the confusion and panic setting in aboard, and also because the auxiliary engines were started in the faint hope of bringing the ship into shallower water before the list increased.

7.   After the accident, Mr. Selvino Sornesi was forced to leave the board of the Italia yard.

But because of political interference, he received a still higher and more remunerative position as chairman of Finmare (an organization for industrial and economic oversight of the four big yards subsidized by the Italian State—Lloyd Trietino, Italia, Tirrenia, and Adriatica—and of smaller yards such as Partenopea for the isles in the Bay of Naples, etc.), while the chairman of the Italian Shipping Registry (R.I.N.), Admiral Barone, and the inexperienced and corrupt technicians in the Merchant Fleet Ministry and afterwards also the cabinet chief and deputy cabinet chief in the Merchant Fleet Ministry were dismissed from their posts.

8.   The Italian special board of inquiry, unlawfully appointed by the Merchant Fleet minister on the occasion of the loss of the *Andrea Doria*, after a year's investigation and after having carried out all possible theoretical studies on a scale model of the *Andrea Doria* (14 meters in length and built for the purpose) still did not know what to decide, for the following reasons:

(a) As regards the seamanship part (radar reading, maneuvering etc.) at the moment of danger and upon collision, all the facts militate against Captain Calamai, who in particular accepted command of the vessel even though he knew beforehand of all the shortcomings in its construction.

But the ministers of the Merchant Fleet and of the navy were absolutely unwilling to allow any fault whatsoever to be found on the part of the Italian vessel, or to reveal the responsibility incumbent upon the commissioner for emigration, Major Giuseppe Campo, who ignominiously fled from the vessel to save himself before the others right after the collision took place, thereby contributing to the panic among the other members of the company, with all the consequences already known to have followed.

(b) The board of inquiry knows that the Swedes declared that for their part, they would not make any official investigation regarding the collision between the two vessels, and that they would approve without reservation the judgment that the American court will hand down in accordance with applicable international convention.

(c) The Ansaldo company in Genoa, who built the *Andrea Doria*, allegedly declared itself unwilling to accept, even indirectly, any liability in the matter of shortcomings of the vessel, and otherwise threatened, in order to protect its international good name, to raise a big scandal and publish the entire dossier in its possession with drawings and plans for the vessel that were

drawn up and checked by the
inexperienced and corrupt technicians
at the Italia yard, in the Italian
Shipping Registry and in the Merchant
Marine Ministry

9.   This is therefore what the Italian board
of inquiry's pronouncement—when it completes
its work (with a high per diem
allowance)—will in all probability come out
with, in concert with the two ministries
(merchant fleet and navy) and because they
cannot do otherwise owing to given
instructions: an indictment in general terms
against Captain Calamai for faults committed,
reading as follows: "By reason of excessive
speed during foggy weather."

August 1957

(Translation by Translation Aces, Inc.)

```
ICZ1399

SGB358 GOTEBORG 61/60 21 1727

NORDBORG HEMLAND NEW YORK

CONSIDER VERY IMPORTANT IF YOU CAN FIND OUT WHETHER WATER-TYPE DOOR
FITTED BETWEEN AUXILIARY ENGINE ROOM AND PIPE TUNNEL SITUATED BETWEEN
FRAMES 146 AND 173 BELOW D DECK STOP ALTERNATIVELY IF COMPLETELY OPEN
OR CLOSED STOP IF NOT SHOWN ON DRAWINGS PERHAPS POSSIBILITY EXISTS
FIND OUT ON CRISTOFORO COLOMBO DURING SNAMES MEETING ONBOARD
WEDNESDAY 26

GREETINGS

CHRISTIANSSON
```

The question of why *Andrea Doria* sank—and sank the way that she did—would have played a crucial role at a possible trial in New York. When the technicians of Swedish America Line studied a somewhat blurred drawing regarding the engine room of *Andrea Doria,* they began to suspect that a watertight door was missing between the generator room and the long tunnel which led to the stem of the ship. Perhaps this was the reason why *Andrea Doria* sank.

The efforts that were made in order to answer this question were reminiscent of a spy novel. One opportunity to solve the mystery about the possibly non-existent watertight door appeared on September 26—two months after the sinking of *Andrea Doria*—when her sister ship, *Cristoforo Colombo,* docked in New York. *Cristoforo Colombo* was an exact duplicate of *Andrea Doria.*

Members of SNAME, an organization of American naval architects and marine engineers, were scheduled to meet on board. A telegram from the technical director of Swedish America Line was sent from Gothenburg to New York with instructions that the group was to investigate whether there was any watertight door between the generator room and the tunnel.

J. Lyell Wilson, retained by Swedish America Line in respect of issues of construction and stability, went to inspect the areas in question himself, and he stated in a telegram and more extensively later in a letter the following:

"There were no doors of any kind."

This was a very important piece of information for the future and answered the question why *Andrea Doria* sank—she was full of water from bow to stern! (Translation by Magnus Jansson.)

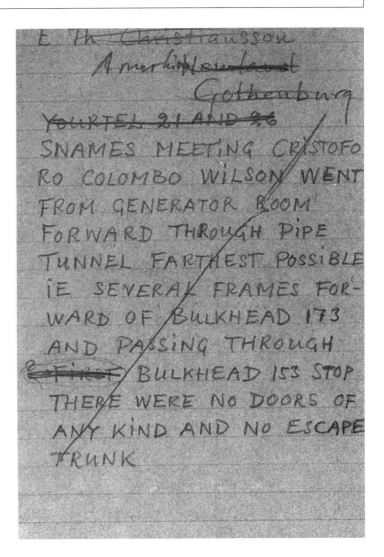

Andrea Doria's profile and bottom deck plan

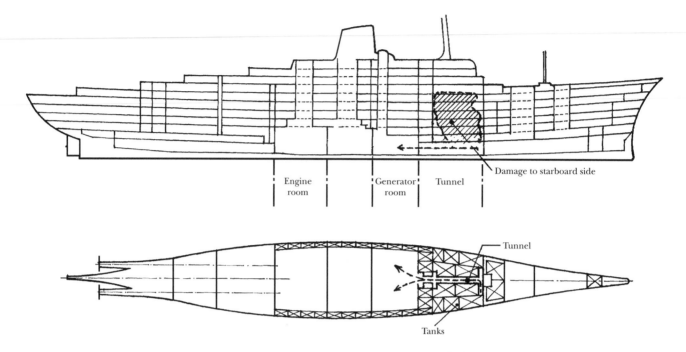

Engine room   Generator room   Tunnel

Damage to starboard side

Tunnel

Tanks

The hull in the area of the empty tanks was demolished and water streamed in through the tunnel in the generator room.

The damage to *Andrea Doria* occurred at her most vulnerable point. If the damage had occurred at just about any other point—engine room or boiler room—*Andrea Doria* probably would have remained afloat.

But when the starboard tanks filled with five hundred tons of water and the port tanks were nearly empty, the port side was elevated and *Andrea Doria* experienced an 18° list.

A flood of seawater rushed into the generator room and filled the starboard side. *Andrea Doria's* list therefore increased rapidly. Water later streamed over the watertight bulkheads and up to the A deck and also through the ventilators on the lower deck as they had not been closed.

CHAPTER 20

One Day in Rome—
Opening *Andrea Doria*'s Safe

A large buoy flashing its light above the gray waves of the Atlantic near Nantucket Island has indicated the location of *Andrea Doria* for many years. As is traditional with a sunken ship, more or less romanticized rumors are often spread regarding the treasures on board. Close to *Andrea Doria*'s location, the American steamship *Republic* went down in 1909 while heading from New York to Gibraltar. It was said she had a cargo of gold worth millions, but this claim has never been proved.

Andrea Doria has been no exception when it comes to the rumors concerning great treasure on board; after all, she was one of the most luxurious ships in the world at that time. Of course, her passenger list included many poor emigrants, but it also showed a great number of rich people who could be expected to have brought along large sums of money as well as gold and diamonds. From the start, people were talking about *Andrea Doria*'s supply of wines and liquors, not to mention the invaluable works of art in all of her lounges and salons.

It was also believed that the passengers had deposited gold, Chinese porcelain, sterling silver, and much else that could only be imagined in the safe in the chief purser's office. Whether or not all this was to be found in the safe was another story. When *Andrea Doria* collided, it was the last evening before arrival in New York. It is very unlikely the passengers, except in unusual circumstances, would have planned to withdraw their valuables so late in the evening. Hence, it is quite probable that the safe had been emptied before the collision with *Stockholm*.

The ship, together with her appointments, was worth a great deal. It was estimated that some bronze sculptures and a silver registration plate would bring in about $250,000 for those who succeeded in recovering these treasures from the bottom of the sea.

Among other objects deemed possible to save were an anchor and two bronze propellers worth $35,000 each. Peter Gimbel—a very skillful amateur diver and heir to the Gimbel department store fortune in the United States—and Joseph Fox dove down to *Andrea Doria* the day after she sank. They returned with a series of black-and-white photos that were published in *Life* magazine. Subsequently, *Life* organized an expedition which included Gimbel to make a photo documentary in color.

It was a much-publicized expedition, mainly because of what could be the spectacular return of possessions to *Andrea Doria's* passengers. Shoes found their owners; Justine Messina got her ocean-drenched suitcase back, and so on.

Over the years, Gimbel's bold diving inspired many others to follow his example. For Gimbel himself that first descent started an almost obsessive fascination with *Andrea Doria.* Neither he nor any other diver brought up the treasures still mentioned in the rumors, and today the ship itself can be regarded as worthless considering the expense that would be involved in salvaging her.

Stena Metall, one of the world's biggest scrap metal companies, stated: "The value of the wreck, except for what might be found in her safe and other equipment of sentimental value, should be something like 5 million Swedish krona. We would not be interested even if we got *Andrea Doria* for free, and even if it was practically possible to raise her."

So there appear to be few economic possibilities at present to bring the Italian luxury liner to the surface, either whole or in part. On the other hand, it will always be regarded as an accomplishment to salvage loose objects and even heavier things—for example, a small safe.

Andrea Doria has been called the divers' Mount Everest. She is now a ghost ship, overgrown by algae and partly shrouded with trawler nets that have become caught in the wreck.

Naturally, sharks and treacherous currents present a great danger for adventurous divers, but one may nevertheless be sure that quite a number will risk their lives.

To have "trod the deck" of *Andrea Doria* lying 70 meters below the surface so many years after her loss is something to tell one's children and grandchildren.

In the summer of 1981, twenty-five years after *Andrea Doria* went down, Peter Gimbel found himself once again at the wreck. He was assisted by thirty-two helpers and a diving bell on board the salvage vessel *Sea Level.* The goal of the expedition was a safe belonging to Banco di Roma.

After a number of difficulties had been overcome, the safe was lifted onto *Sea Level* and subsequently placed in the shark aquarium in New York. There it lay for a couple of years, until bubbles were seen around its door. The experts believed the bubbles indicated some sort of fermentation process, which probably started because the water in the shark tank was too warm.

The safe was moved to a cooler aquarium without sharks but with human guards on duty in the building around the clock. There it lay, wrapped up like a Christmas present but with heavy chains instead of ribbons, until August 16, 1984. Then it was opened as a much-publicized event broadcast live by both American and Italian television.

The Italians had decided early on to produce a memorial program about *Andrea Doria* in connection with the opening of the safe. The program was to be anchored by the "Italian David Frost," the well-known and talented television celebrity Alberto La Volpe, who had two and a half hours at his disposal.

Except for previously recorded footage on *Andrea Doria*—her launching, her maiden voyage, life on board, and arrival in New York—the program was presented as a hearing.

Behind the anchorman there was an enormous enlargement of a photograph of *Andrea Doria* taken just as her stack sank into the Atlantic. One of the side screens showed Italian Line's versions of the ships' courses, and also what was supposed to be

Swedish America Line's, in addition to the course of events in general.

The investigation panel included a large number of people with connections to Italian Line and *Andrea Doria*. The mates were there as well as the engineers, an attorney, the chief purser, the ship's physician, and representatives of the passengers and crew.

In this group, where everyone spoke for Italian Line's version of the collision and the sinking of *Andrea Doria,* there was one single Swede, Johan-Ernst Carstens-Johannsen, third mate on *Stockholm* when the collision occurred. Italian television had gone to great effort to persuade Carstens to appear on this program, which was judged to be of special interest to the Italian public at large. Carstens said:

> There is no doubt that I had reservations about appearing, but I finally decided it was necessary for someone to present Swedish America Line's version of the collision. I decided to stick strictly to what had been revealed while I was being heard in New York.
>
> Only when I arrived in Rome did I learn that it was to be a documentary program, but I received no information about who was showing up or in what atmosphere the broadcast was to take place. In reply to my queries, I was told the studio had not yet been constructed. A half-hour before the program was to begin, I was picked up at my hotel, and then I got to know a little about the setup.
>
> When I arrived in the studio, I noticed immediately there was more than one person from *Andrea Doria*'s crew who was not overjoyed at my participation. Chief Engineer Giovanni Cordera seemed upset to see me and refused to say hello, but he calmed down after the program. After all, he would have been one of the witnesses Swedish America Line's attorney, Charles Haight, would have leaned on hardest if the hearing in New York had not been broken off.

At the outset, the program was dominated by live coverage of the opening of *Andrea Doria*'s safe. After some difficulty the door was opened, and it appeared, as expected, that it was a typical small safe used for currency exchanges. It contained lire, dollars, stamps, and so forth.

Carstens stated:

> That safe had absolutely nothing to do with the big safe in the purser's office, which was surely emptied before the ship sank.

Italian television had a reporter in place in New York, and he did a number of special interviews with both Peter Gimbel and his wife, Elga Andersen. As the safe was gradually emptied, they both seemed increasingly disillusioned. The anticipated discovery of gold and diamonds failed to materialize. The contents were bundles of dollar and lire notes, which the seawater had converted into something that almost resembled clumps of oil.

On the American television program, Elga Andersen, who had participated in several of her husband's expeditions, said spontaneously that she wished *Andrea Doria*'s safe had never been opened, that it had been left submerged in the aquarium to tickle the fancies of visitors.

"It feels as if some kind of curse lies over *Andrea Doria*," she said, and told how a violent storm had surprised the expedition just as the safe was being salvaged. "It came like a bolt from the blue," said Andersen. "The same thing happened when the safe was to be opened in the aquarium. A lightning storm moved in over New York and lightning struck just outside the aquarium."

Elga Andersen was right—the mystery surrounding *Andrea Doria*'s safe would have been preserved had it never been opened. Instead, the opening was an anticlimax, and neither Gimbel nor Andersen could manage to appear enthusiastic as the waterlogged notes were lifted up with specially constructed shovels.

It had cost Gimbel $2 million to salvage the safe. The total value of all the banknotes was $20,000. The New York Customs

Office took a look at the safe and its contents but decided that no import duty could be levied on its arrival in New York from international waters. Old bills and a rusty safe were not worth the trouble, said the chief customs officer.

Yet, Gimbel and Andersen decided to make some kind of profit from the old bills. They were dried, sealed in plastic, and put on sale for $300 apiece. Many people have wondered whether bringing up the safe from *Andrea Doria* was really such a great achievement.

Carstens related:

Of course, it was impressive to dive down and do the job with the technology they used. But if you compare it with how people work, for example, out in the offshore oil fields, it was very amateurish. They went about it in 1950s fashion, and I'm sure that a diving team from today's offshore companies using modern equipment would have salvaged the safe in very short order.

After the live broadcast showed the opening of *Andrea Doria*'s safe, the "hearing" in Rome opened with the anchorman reading aloud, word for word, Captain Calamai's defense statement before the preliminary hearing began in New York. Carstens explained:

When that was done, I realized that nobody knew what had happened after the hearing. Swedish America Line's attorney, Charles Haight, had more or less destroyed Captain Calamai as a witness, so now we got a replay of the defense statement, and I really thought it was wrong to honor the memory of Captain Calamai in that way. After all, it was a result of the orders given on *Andrea Doria*'s bridge that she collided with *Stockholm* and then sank.

Captain Calamai's various actions on the bridge were next defended primarily by Luigi Oneto, who was first mate at the time. He had been on the bridge when *Andrea Doria* passed Nantucket but had gone off watch before the collision. First Mate Oneto confirmed that at that time, there had been thick fog but had

difficulty explaining why *Andrea Doria* did not proceed at a greatly reduced speed since she was a turbine-propelled ship with a very long braking distance.

It turned into a real confrontation program which was translated into English for my benefit. I certainly couldn't complain about the neutrality of the anchorman, Alberto La Volpe. All I had to do was lift my eyebrows to get his attention, and I did it often during the long deluge of Italian words.

Most of the representatives of *Andrea Doria*'s crew had the chance to speak, so I really had to concentrate and offer quick replies. My advantage was that I had been present the whole time from the sighting of *Andrea Doria* as a distant radar echo until I could look into *Doria*'s bridge from *Stockholm*. None of the other participants in the program could claim that, except for Third Mate Eugenio Giannini, who suddenly entered the discussion near the end of the program via telephone.

Giannini came up with the bizarre assertion that I had confused *Andrea Doria* for the *Nantucket* lightship, after which the conversation was quickly cut off.

The program had been given a lot of advance publicity in the big Italian newspapers, which devoted whole pages to trying to explain the course of the collision.

When I went for a walk in Rome the next day, I was amazed at the impact the broadcast obviously had. What was remarkable was that I was so recognizable. People came up and pointed at me as though they wanted to make sure I was not a ghost. They addressed me as "El Commendore" and offered to buy me food and drink. What they said I don't really know, but everyone was friendly and nobody acted in a threatening way.

When I went into the Gucci shop by the Spanish Steps, the proprietor gathered his personnel and thanked me for standing up against so many people from Italian Line; he thought it was unforgivable to put up one man against all of those. They all said they were really grateful to find out at last what had really happened when *Andrea Doria* and *Stockholm* collided.

Rarely have I encountered so many pleasant and understanding people as I did after that television appearance in Rome.

CHAPTER 21

Carstens: "I Will Never Regret That Maneuver"

Johan-Ernst Carstens-Johannsen, *Stockholm's* third mate at the time of the tragedy, hailed from the Swedish province of Skåne. When author Algot Mattsson interviewed him in 1986, it was not hard to imagine that Carstens was essentially the same person who had sole responsibility on *Stockholm's* bridge on the night of July 25 and 26, 1956, thirty years before the publication of this book in Sweden.

Mattsson: Did the collision between *Stockholm* and *Andrea Doria* alter your life?

Carstens: Hardly, in the sense of being psychologically shattered by what happened. I can claim with a clear conscience that I have never lain awake at night agonizing over what happened to me. It was, of course, a catastrophe that I wish fate might have spared me.

The curious thing is that I didn't reflect very much about what I had experienced during the period immediately following the accident. Nor did I care very much about what was written in the newspapers, although what appeared there was very often wrong.

It's really only in recent years that I have become irritated when the same idiocies are repeated time after time. Perhaps I have only myself to blame for stubbornly refusing to speak, to explain, to set the record straight. I've often thought about it, but after mature reflection, I've decided that it would have been pointless to try to explain.

Of course, Swedish America Line did not forbid me to talk about the collision, but I realized they preferred to have the world forget entirely about this tragic event in the company's history, so when the management pointed out to me they hoped the squabbling would end, it was an indirect way of cautioning me to keep quiet.

But, naturally, it's often been hard to hold my tongue when the newspapers keep on writing the same old erroneous stories on the occasion of every anniversary since *Andrea Doria* went down. Soon it will be thirty years.

Mattsson: Have you tried to forget the event?

Carstens: Obviously, one doesn't want to be constantly reminded about a tragic

137

incident in one's life, but it hasn't always been so easy to shake off that shadow.

I recall when I have met people and have been introduced as Captain Carstens-Johannsen with the comment, "He's the one who ran into *Andrea Doria*." That's no laughing matter! Just as though that was my greatest accomplishment in life.

Mattsson: Have you told your children about the collision?

Carstens: Not very much actually, but when they got old enough to read, they nearly read the first book to pieces: Alvin Moscow's *Collision Course* published in 1959 is pretty much worn out.

Mattsson: Have you talked much with your wife about the accident?

Carstens: Not much. I don't go around repeating unpleasant experiences. That's not my style, nor my wife's. It can happen when I am reminded by the press.

Mattsson: How does it feel to be reminded about it once again, to have to revert to what happened, both the collision itself and the aftermath of the hearing in New York?

Carstens: No problem. After all this time, I have really achieved perspective on what happened, and that's why I've been happy to talk about it all now.

After all, a catastrophe such as that means tragedy for many people, yet amongst all the misery there were also truly comical features. To talk about them, too, is not to diminish all the suffering that followed in the wake of the collision. But in life, as in death, there are both shadows and sunbeams.

Mattsson: Have you ever regretted your final maneuvers prior to the collision with *Andrea Doria*?

Carstens: Not for a minute! Naturally, I have often gone through the entire course of events, but I have always come to the same conclusion: I turned in the right direction.

As it was, *Andrea Doria* was on our port side, but even if we had approached head-on, I would have chosen the same final maneuver.

As everyone knows, that's the law of the sea.

Nor was I alone on the bridge. There were three other men, and before the collision, they all saw what I saw. So it wasn't a matter of making something up in retrospect.

Mattsson: And the fog, what about that?

Carstens: There was absolutely no fog in our immediate area, but from experience with these waters, I checked constantly. There were no wisps of fog shading the lights at the top of the masts. Visibility was good, and we didn't have to reduce *Stockholm*'s speed because she could stop within 350 meters. It was of course worrisome that the current had driven us about 3 nautical miles north of our original course, but that had absolutely no significance relating to how the collision came about.

Mattsson: A short time earlier, *Nantucket* lightship had been moved to a location somewhat southwest of her original position. Did that have any significance?

Carstens: Not for us. We had received information about that, and the light's new location had been marked on our chart. But *Andrea Doria*, which went farther north than we did, must have just squeezed past it. As a matter of fact, it's been the fate of that light to be rammed by ships from Europe approaching New York in heavy fog.

Mattsson: Would you have welcomed a proper trial?

Carstens: No doubt about it. Of course, I considered myself completely exonerated by the preliminary hearing in New York and the settlement that was reached in London, but nothing can compare with being declared innocent in a court of law.

For economic reasons watched over by the insurance companies, and for concerns about the marketplace dictated by Swedish America Line and Italian Line, I had to content myself with being right, without the luxury of having it certified in court.

Years ago I accepted that fact, even with some misgivings. Today, with all the facts of the case on the table, I have no misgivings.

Author's Epilogue

July 1956—a bygone time in the history of passenger travel. The memory of the great collision between *Stockholm* and *Andrea Doria* has of course lingered on over the decades, but the golden age of the great liners on the North Atlantic is gone forever.

Enthusiastic tourists and emigrants no longer crowd the piers along the Hudson River. Only a few times a year do passenger ships depart for and arrive from Europe.

In the months following the collision between *Stockholm* and *Andrea Doria*, the great ships came and went like ferryboats, transporting tens of thousands of passengers every week. It was the busiest season for voyages between the United States and Europe.

Stockholm returned to Pier 97 on July 27, 1956, the day following the collision. On the same day, United States Line's *America* departed for Southampton and Bremerhaven, and Greek Line's *Olympic* left for harbors in the Mediterranean. On the following day, Saturday, July 28, it was the turn of Cunard Line's old beauty, *Mauritania*—she sailed off to Southampton.

During the next week, between July 31 and August 5, no fewer than twelve ships

left New York Harbor. Passenger traffic across the North Atlantic had increased tremendously since the end of World War II. It peaked in 1957, one year after *Andrea Doria* went down, when no fewer than 1,037,289 people traveled by ship between Europe and North America. Yet, just one year later, more travelers elected airplanes over ships. By 1960, jet planes had definitively won the battle for the North Atlantic, and by the end of that decade, only 4 percent of transatlantic travelers sailed the seas.

The many majestic ships on the North Atlantic could be written off as part of a glorious but vanished chapter in the history of maritime passenger travel, though they did not disappear for good. Many of them were built with an eye to the steadily growing cruise liner market, and they had gradually been transferred to this profitable enterprise. Such was the case, for example, for Swedish America Line's two last luxury liners, *Kungsholm* and *Gripsholm*, both of which were regarded as among the finest of their kind in the whole world.

Hence, when Swedish America Line was shut down in 1975, the ships were sold to companies that knew how to take advantage of their fine reputations. Both *Gripsholm* and *Kungsholm* competed very successfully on the cruise market for many years.

Kungsholm, rechristened *Sea Princess* and owned by the P&O Line, resumed round–the-world cruises. *Gripsholm* was refurbished at the end of 1985 for $13,000,000. As previously stated, *Stockholm,* later rechristened *Völkerfreundschaft,* was purchased from the East German government and put into service as a cruise ship.

Italian Line, which had become known throughout the world in connection with the loss of *Andrea Doria,* had been created in 1932 during Mussolini's reign. The company was formed by the merging of three leading Italian shipping companies—Navigazione Generale Italiana, the Cosulich Line, and Lloyd Sabaudo.

Italian Line operated passenger traffic on both the North and South Atlantic, but the sister ships *Andrea Doria* and *Cristoforo Colombo,* both operating between Mediterranean harbors and New York, were the company's "crown jewels."

Immediately after the sinking of *Andrea Doria,* Italian Line announced that it was going to build "a new *Andrea Doria.*" The new ship was finished in 1960 but was christened *Leonardo da Vinci,* not *Andrea Doria.* Before North Atlantic traffic died out, the Italian fleet was provided with two more large passenger ships. They were *Michelangelo* and *Rafaello,* sister ships in the 45,000-ton class with exquisite appointments.

Yet the great ships, however luxuriously equipped and comfortable, were doomed to disappear. Italian Line's service ceased in 1976, and its fleet was split up. *Andrea Doria's* sister ship, *Cristoforo Colombo,* ended her days in a scrap yard in Taiwan in 1982.

Millions of people traveled between America and Europe during the era of the great ships. All of them had, and some still have, strong memories of "their" ship.

Two in particular will live down through the generations—*Titanic* and *Andrea Doria.*

Editors' Epilogue

Despite the passage of almost a half century since the event, the collision of *Stockholm* and *Andrea Doria* in July 1956 is not forgotten. In fact, *Stockholm* is still sailing as the cruise ship *Valtur Prima*, ironically under the Italian flag with Italian officers. With the help of Frank Duffy, the editors boarded the ship and met her Italian master on April 23, 1997, the date of the ship's maiden call in New York under the Italian flag. The master knew well the vessel's history.

In Cape Cod recently, the local newspaper, the *Cape Cod Times*, featured an article entitled "Newsman Recalls Andrea Doria Tragedy for TV," which describes the event as "the last great shipwreck of the golden age of transatlantic luxury liners." The article mentions that freelance photographer Bill Quinn of Orleans, Massachusetts, had photographed the ships just after the collision. The History Channel was to air the story in January of 2002.

Also, the *Philadelphia Inquirer* for Sunday, August 12, 2001, contained a major article about twelve divers who dove to the wreck of *Andrea Doria*, which "lies in 240 feet of water 50 miles south of Nantucket." The article was a review of the just-published book, *Adventure and Death: Diving the Andrea Doria*, by Kenneth F. McMurray, which states, "Each ship had radar and each saw the other speeding ahead—which makes the tragedy all the more mysterious."

Another book published in 2001 focuses on the rescue effort that saved so many of *Andrea Doria*'s passengers and crew. All of this suggests that the collision and its cause are still of interest.

Alvin Moscow, author of *Collision Course*, stated to the *New York Times* regarding the collision:

> Exactly why the two ships collided in open water when they had seen each other on radar remains a mystery. The legal issues were settled out of court, so there is scant testimony.

It is the editors' hope that this book will help solve the mystery!

Editors' Legal Opinion

One Possible Outcome of the *Stockholm–Andrea Doria* Case Had It Gone to Trial

Inasmuch as the merits of the *Stockholm–Andrea Doria* collision have not been decided by any court—and never will be—it may be of interest to the reader to have the editors' opinion as to the possible result if the litigation in the United States District Court for the Southern District of New York had not been settled. This opinion is based on the evidence that had been presented during the New York proceedings and further research done in the ensuing years.[1]

It had been obvious to the attorneys from the very beginning that litigation regarding this collision would probably take place in the United States, most likely in the federal court in Manhattan where both the Swedish America Line and the Italian Line maintained offices. Jurisdiction could thus be readily established. United States Federal Court would take jurisdiction over the matter whether the collision occurred in international waters, foreign territorial waters, or domestic waters. See chapter 1, "Basic Principles of Collision Law," in Healy and Sweeney's *Law of Marine Collision,* Cornell Maritime Press, 1998 (hereinafter "Healy and Sweeney").

As noted in the text, under United States maritime law in effect at the time of the collision between *Stockholm* and *Andrea Doria,* if both vessels had been in contributory fault, the damages would be equally divided, except if it had been established that the nations whose flags both vessels were flying had ratified the 1910 International Convention for the Unification of Certain Rules of Law with Respect to Collisions between Vessels (the "1910 Collision Convention"). In that case "the liability of each vessel would be in proportion to the degree

─────────────

1. For their assistance in the preparation of this chapter, Gordon W. Paulsen expresses his appreciation to his partners Nicholas J. Healy, Howard M. McCormack, and William N. France; and his friend Captain Willard F. Searle, USN, retired. None of them has given complete assent to all the opinions expressed herein.

of faults respectively committed" (Article 4). Both Sweden and Italy had ratified the convention long before this collision, but the United States had not (and still hasn't). So United States courts sitting in admiralty would have applied the doctrine of proportional fault if this case had been litigated in the United States, rather than settled. (It should be noted that, while not ratifying the 1910 Collision Convention, the United States now applies the doctrine of proportional fault in collision cases by reason of the decision of the Supreme Court in *United States v Reliable Transfer Co. Inc.*, 421 US 397, 95 S.Ct. 1708, 1975 AMC 541 (1975).)

Although the collision occurred close to the East Coast of the United States, the location was in what would be considered international waters from the standpoint of the rules of navigation.[2] At the time of the collision, the applicable rules were the International Rules for the Prevention of Collisions at Sea (the "International Rules") of 1890.[3]

Both vessels were equipped with radar. It has frequently been held that if a vessel is so equipped, it must be used properly. For example, in *The Nora,* a 1956 English case, the rule was stated by the court:

> . . .[T]he possession of this radar equipment gives the *Westerdam* a great advantage over other vessels which are not similarly equipped; but it brings with it, in my judgment, a concurrent duty to see that intelligent and reasonable use is made of the equipment provided. . .[4]

At the time of the collision, "proper use" of radar included plotting either on a maneuvering board or with a grease pencil on the radarscope itself.[5] Nowadays, most sizable ships are equipped with automatic radar plotting aids (ARPAs), as required by the United States Coast Guard Regulations.[6] Obviously, watchstanding deck officers are required to have proper training in the use of radar. The fact that *Andrea Doria* was operating in thick fog at almost full speed without plotting shows that her navigators did not understand or appreciate radar. Her plotting boards had been stored in a closet.

ALLEGATIONS OF CONTRIBUTORY FAULT OF *ANDREA DORIA*

1. Those navigating *Andrea Doria* had not been properly trained in the use of radar, and therefore did not use it properly.

Although *Andrea Doria* was equipped with radar, her master and some of her officers had either inadequate training or no instructions at all for its use. Incidentally, at the time of the collision it was not possible to use ship-to-ship radio between ships whose identities or radio call letters were not known. In any event, no one aboard realized *Andrea Doria* was on a collision course with *Stockholm*. The navigators of *Andrea Doria* failed to understand that collision could not be avoided without proper action by *both* vessels. Under the circumstances, *Andrea Doria* not only was in violation of Rule 18 of the International Rules then in effect (see below) but also did not apply principles of good seaman-

---

2. See J. W. Griffin, *The American Law of Collision* (hereinafter Griffin, *Collision*), §§ 302.1-302.15 (1949).

3. 1910 International Convention for the Unification of Certain Rules with Respect to Collisions between Vessels, reprinted in Healy and Sweeney at 544 (1998). See also, F. Wiswall, 6 *Benedict on Admiralty* (hereinafter *Benedict*) Doc. 3-2 (7th ed. 2000).

4. *The Nora* [1956] 1 Lloyd's Rep. 617, 625–6 (1956). See also *In Re Waterstand Marine Ltd.*, 1991 AMC 1784, 1797–9 (E.D. Pa. 1988) (improper training and use of ARPA caused collision and precluded shipowner from limiting liability).

5. Healy and Sweeney, 116.

6. Ibid., 117.

ship. This failure to recognize the ships' relative positions was the major contributory cause of the collision.

In the relatively early days of radar, the failure to appreciate that a radar screen is not the same as a television screen—as well as unfamiliarity with "relative motion" (i.e., the vessel indicated by a pip on the radar screen, as well as the vessel on which the radar screen is located, are both moving)—caused some navigators to have a false sense of security. As a result, some ship collisions, such as this one, have been described as "radar assisted."[7] If *Andrea Doria* had not been equipped with radar, the collision may not have happened.

2. *Andrea Doria* turned to port rather than starboard.

International Rule 18, which was in force in 1956, provided for vessels in sight of one another:

> When two steam vessels are meeting end on, or nearly end on, so as to involve risk of collision, each shall alter her course to *starboard* so that each may pass on the port side of the other [emphasis supplied].[8]

Andrea Doria's port rudder order given just before the collision was *the* proximate cause of the collision. Had the watch officer on *Andrea Doria*'s bridge obeyed the rules and properly used radar, he would have known that the port rudder order was wrong.

If *Andrea Doria* had altered course to starboard when the vessels came in sight of each other, as did *Stockholm*, the collision may not even have occurred.

3. Those in charge of *Andrea Doria* failed to moderate her speed in view of reduced visibility.

Andrea Doria failed to proceed at a moderate speed in violation of Rule 16 of the International Rules,[9] which required that vessels in fog, mist, falling snow, or heavy rainstorms should proceed at a moderate speed, having careful regard to the prevailing circumstances and conditions.

"Moderate speed" has been defined as one which would make it possible for a ship to stop dead in the water within her "share of the visibility." This has been held to mean half the limit of visibility, on the theory that if she stopped her engines immediately upon hearing the fog signal of another vessel directly ahead that was also proceeding at moderate speed, collision could be averted.

This definition is highly theoretical in that neither vessel can know the stopping power of the other; but it is a useful rule, especially where, as here, one ship is in fog and the other is in an area of visibility but is on the edge of the fogbank.

4. *Andrea Doria* failed to replenish ballast water in the course of her voyage to New York and failed to compensate for the weight of the fuel used during the voyage.

Those in charge of *Andrea Doria* had failed to replenish her ballast water as it was being used and failed to take into consideration that she had largely used up her fuel by July 25, 1956, with the result that she was top-heavy, and there was no way to correct the list which developed after the collision.

In fact, press photographs of the starboard list that *Andrea Doria* developed immediately after the collision attracted the

---

7. See the article by Gustaf Ahrne reprinted as appendix B hereto.
8. See Griffin, *Collision* 669.
9. Ibid., 668.

attention of the United States House of Representatives, which appointed a committee with the task of investigating whether *Andrea Doria* complied with SOLAS and its requirements with respect to watertight compartments and stability. As noted in the text and in appendix B, the report of the committee found that *Andrea Doria* just barely met the requirements of the 1948 convention as to watertight compartments. She met the stability requirement, but only on condition that she was adequately ballasted.

Before the preliminary hearing commenced in New York in September 1956, the attorneys on *Stockholm*'s legal team had concluded that *Andrea Doria* should have survived the collision and that capsizing as she did was indicative of the fact that she had not been properly managed.

Early on in *Andrea Doria*'s career, it had become apparent to those in charge of her that as she consumed fuel and water, she needed to compensate for the weight change in order to maintain stability. She needed to take on ballast to match the weight of the water and fuel used during the earlier part of the voyage. This ballast adjustment could have been taken care of by proper planning and management during each voyage. In fact, it was a condition of her seaworthy certificate that she replenish ballast as needed. As mentioned in the first chapter of this book, during her maiden voyage she experienced a sudden and violent wind broadside and recorded a list of 28°, which indicated then that her stability was not up to par. (The same sort of thing had happened to *Stockholm*, but not to the same extent.)

Thus, the failure to replenish ballast, coupled with *Andrea Doria*'s basic instability

(see below), made it impossible to correct her fatal list.

5. *Andrea Doria* was designed and built with defects which made her unseaworthy.

The design and construction of *Andrea Doria*, to the personal knowledge of her owner, were defective. Contrary to the requirements of SOLAS, reprinted at 6 *Benedict* Doc. 14-1, she was designed and built with a longitudinal tunnel which was so constructed that once that tunnel was pierced, *Andrea Doria* could not remain afloat for any appreciable length of time.

As was known by the parties to the litigation commenced in the United States District Court for the Southern District of New York in 1956, Charles Haight had arranged for *Andrea Doria*'s almost-exact sister ship, *Cristoforo Colombo,* to be inspected by J. Lyell Wilson, a distinguished naval architect and member of SNAME on October 7, 1956.[10] His report of inspection is included in this book as appendix C.

The inspection had been urged by Haight to fortify the argument that *Andrea Doria* was basically unseaworthy from the start and *that* was the reason she sank so soon after the collision. Wilson pointed out that "the structural arrangements in the compartment of *Andrea Doria*'s subdivision with which the collision was primarily involved . . . violated the letter and intent of the Safety of Life at Sea Convention (SOLAS) as interpreted by the United States Coast Guard Regulations for Passenger Vessels (C.G. 256 November 19, 1952) [and that] the collision happened at just the right place to prove lack of proper stability and an ap-

---

10. Those invited to the survey of *Cristoforo Colombo* included Eugene Underwood, Kenneth Volk, Charles S. Haight, Jr., and Gordon W. Paulsen. Volk and Paulsen are past presidents of The Maritime Law Association of the United States and are still active in the practice of maritime law.

parent design error on the *Andrea Doria* [page 6]." Wilson further concluded "that lack of stability was a major cause of the sinking of *Andrea Doria* [page 8]."[11]

Gary Gentile in his book *Andrea Doria: Dive to an Era* wrote of a "nagging" thought that Elga Anderson, Gimbel's partner in the diving expeditions to the wreck of *Andrea Doria*, had about the ship's design. *Andrea Doria* was supposed to have been designed never to list more than 15°. In fact she listed immediately to 18° and eventually much more.[12]

Gentile writes about the fact that in 1981 divers discovered a break, never before suspected, which led out to the sea from the generator room. The divers observed that *Andrea Doria*'s hull had been "split open like a ripe watermelon. . . . With three compartments torn open by the collision, the luxury liner had suffered a blow with which she was unable to cope. The mystery of her sinking had at last been solved."[13]

ALLEGATIONS OF CONTRIBUTORY FAULT OF *STOCKHOLM*

1. *Stockholm* should have sounded a signal for a port-to-port passing and should have taken other precautions to prevent a collision.

Stockholm failed to realize that *Andrea Doria*, contrary to Rule 18 of the International Rules, contemplated an unorthodox starboard-to-starboard passing with *Stockholm*. In fact, Captain Calamai had decided on a starboard-to-starboard passing from the moment he first saw the pip of *Stockholm* on his radar.

Both *Stockholm* and *Andrea Doria* were equipped with radar and thus each vessel was aware of the presence of the other before either vessel could be seen visually. *Stockholm*'s third mate, who was on watch on the bridge, kept close tabs on the pip of the approaching vessel by plotting. He thought that the two ships, as Rule 18 prescribed, were going to pass one another port-to-port in relatively close proximity, and they would have if *Andrea Doria* had not turned to port. As the other ship came into view out of the fog, everybody concerned on *Stockholm* suddenly realized that *Andrea Doria*, contrary to prior expectations, had been planning on a starboard-to-starboard passing. If *Stockholm* had sounded the signal for a port-to-port passing, it would have alerted *Andrea Doria* to the fact that *Stockholm* was dangerously close. Even at the last moment, *Andrea Doria* could have taken some action to avoid collision, other than the fatal port turn.

The article by Gustaf Ahrne (appendix B) explains how a vessel approaching another vessel on an almost head-to-head course could easily come to an erroneous conclusion as to how the vessels would pass each other, especially if the courses had not been plotted. If *Andrea Doria*'s navigators had been plotting, they would have realized that the starboard-to-starboard passing which was being contemplated by *Andrea Doria* not only would be contrary to the rules but, under the circumstances, would be fatal!

There was some risk that *Stockholm* might be held at fault for failure to sound a signal that she was turning to starboard, and that failure could be held to be a contributory cause of the collision. There was also the

---

11. Wilson's complete report has been examined by William N. France, partner at Healy and Baillie. In addition to being an attorney, France graduated from the Webb Institute as a naval architect and is a member of SNAME. He concurs with the language and conclusions of Wilson's report.

12. Gary Gentile, *Dive to an Era* (hereinafter Gentile, *Dive*) (Philadelphia: Gary Gentile Productions, 1989).

13. Ibid., 75.

risk that the speed of *Stockholm,* while less than that of *Andrea Doria* and even considering the high braking power of her diesel engine, could be considered excessive under the circumstances if the case had come to trial. The possibility existed even though *Stockholm* had not been in fog. *Stockholm* knew (or should have known) from her radar observations that a vessel *(Andrea Doria)* was approaching from an area of fog and that it was incumbent upon her *(Stockholm)* to reduce speed, to take precautions to avoid collision, to navigate with extreme care, and to sound appropriate signals.

LIMITATION OF SHIPOWNER'S LIABILITY

On August 7, 1956, the owner of *Stockholm* filed a petition in the United States District Court for the Southern District of New York to limit its liability, if any, to the value of the vessel and her pending freight (her earnings from the voyage on which the casualty occurred) pursuant to the Limitation of Shipowners' Liability Act (the "Limitation Act") 46 USC §183 *et seq.* (2001). The owner of *Andrea Doria* filed a similar petition at about the same time. The rationale for the Limitation Act (which is available to foreign as well as domestic shipowners) is stated in *Rautbord v. Ehmann,* 190 F.2d 533, 537 (7th Cir. 1951):

> The statutory provision for limitation of liability, enacted in light of the maritime law of modern Europe and of legislation in England, has been broadly and liberally construed in order to achieve its purpose to encourage investments in shipbuilding and to afford an opportunity for determination of claims against a vessel and its owner.

The justification for the statute, which was enacted in 1851 and codified then-existing principles of maritime law, was that shipping is inherently risky, that imposing full liability on a shipowner would discourage investment in shipping, and that it would be unfair to hold a shipowner liable for events that occur on the high seas, beyond the owner's knowledge or control. *See generally* T. Schoenbaum, *Admiralty and Maritime Law,* §15-1 (3d. ed. 2001). Although often criticized, particularly in recent years, the Limitation Act remains in force.

In order for a shipowner to limit liability, the collision or other event for which limitation of liability is sought must have occurred "without the *privity or knowledge* of such owner or owners" [emphasis supplied] 46 USC §183(a).

Because the design of *Andrea Doria* was defective to the knowledge of the owner (i.e., it was within the owner's "privity or knowledge") and its design defects were causally connected with the collision and/or the subsequent sinking, it is the editors' opinion that the owner of *Andrea Doria* would not have been entitled to limit its liability in a United States court. On the other hand, the owner of *Stockholm* would have been entitled to limit its liability because the collision occurred without privity or knowledge of the owner.

The design and construction of *Andrea Doria,* to the personal knowledge of her owner, were defective. *Andrea Doria* could and should have survived the collision. It is the editors' opinion that perhaps the fairest way for a court to deal with the problem of separating the damage due to the collision from the damage caused by her defective design, construction, and management would be to estimate as closely as possible what the cost would have been to repair the damage due to the collision itself, then add the incidental expenses and loss of use, and finally subtract the damages resulting from the vessel's having become a total loss. This would be a herculean task but not an impossible one. *Andrea Doria* would then be entitled to recover her proportional share of damages for the collision itself, but, in the editors' view, not damages resulting from her sinking.[14] (Alternatively, the court could take the design defects into account in apportioning fault.)

CONCLUSION

It is the editors' opinion that the contributory faults of *Andrea Doria* were much more serious than any fault of *Stockholm*. On the other hand, as noted, the Swedish ship *could* have been held at fault, although to a much lesser degree.

The language of Judge Alvin B. Rubin, used in an unrelated case involving a collision between *White Alder* and *Helena*,[15] is singularly applicable to the *Stockholm–Andrea Doria* collision, under the circumstances prevailing on the night of July 25, 1956:

> It is profitless to attempt to weigh fault against fault as if each shortcoming could be measured in some sort of scale. Both vessels were at fault and actively so. The errors of neither were minor. Each vessel committed acts that contributed to the collision. No single act of either can be completely disentangled. But *White Alder*'s unexplained sheer

into the course of *Helena* was the fateful and final act of negligence.

In that case, as in this one, it was the "unexplained sheer" of *Andrea Doria* into the course of *Stockholm* which was the "fateful and final act of negligence." It was never explained in the *Stockholm–Andrea Doria* proceedings in New York why the master of *Andrea Doria* decided to suddenly alter course to port, rather than to starboard as required by Rule 18, so that each vessel could meet and pass on the port side of the other. The "sheer" thus remains unexplained.

It is the editors' opinion that a decision apportioning 70 percent fault to *Andrea Doria* and 30 percent to *Stockholm* would not have been an inappropriate result of the litigation of the merits of the collision. (As a matter of fact, as reported in the *New York Times* of Sunday, October 26, 1980, while no legal determination was ever reached, and the settlement document was never made public, the dispute between the vessel owners and their insurers was secretly settled on the basis of 70 percent fault of *Andrea Doria* and 30 percent fault of *Stockholm*.)

Further, it is the editors' opinion that the claim of *Andrea Doria*'s owner for the loss of *Andrea Doria* would not be allowed. The vessel did not sink because of the collision; the collision was the last of a long series of serious errors. She could and should have survived the collision if she had been better planned, built, and managed.

---

14. See foreword to Gentile, *Dive*, which contains this interesting comment on the *Stockholm–Andrea Doria* collision: "The collision should not have occurred, and the liner should not have sunk." The editors agree.

15. *In Re Sincere Navigation Corp.*, 1976 AMC 2013 (E.D. La. 1976).

REFERENCES

Carrothers, John Carroll. "There Must Have Been a Third Ship" and "The *Andrea Doria–Stockholm* Disaster." *Proceedings,* U.S. Naval Institute.

Cockcroft, A. N., and J. N. F. Lameijer. *A Guide to Collision Avoidance Rules,* 5th ed. Burlington, Mass.: Butterworth-Heinemann, 1996.

Gentile, Gary. *Andrea Doria: Dive to an Era.* Philadelphia: Gary Gentile Productions, 1989.

Healy, Nicholas J., and Joseph C. Sweeney. *The Law of Marine Collision.* Centreville, Md.: Cornell Maritime Press, 1998.

Hoffer, William. *Saved! The Story of the Andrea Doria—the Greatest Sea Rescue in History.* New York: Simon and Schuster, 1979.

Moscow, Alvin. *Collision Course.* New York: Grosset and Dunlap, 1959, 1981.

A Radar Assisted Collision

Captain Gustaf Ahrne

*This article regarding the Stockholm–Andrea Doria case was written in 1972 and published
in the house organ of Sveriges Ångfartygs Assurans Forening (The Swedish Club).
Translated from Swedish by Magnus I. H. Jansson and edited by Nicholas J. Healy.*

THE WORST MARITIME CASUALTY OF ONE HUNDRED YEARS

Many articles and books have been written about the 1956 collision between *Stockholm* and *Andrea Doria*. The most famous book, written by Alvin Moscow, is entitled *Collision Course*. Newspaper articles continue to appear and even today, "nautical persons" try to analyze why the collision happened.

As a major hull and protection underwriter of *Stockholm*, the Swedish Club was very much involved from the outset of the first investigation and up to the final settlement of all claims. Since the nautical aspects of the collision are well known, only some of the major features will be discussed herein. However, we do think our readers would appreciate an account of the settlement agreement regarding the two ships and how this settlement can properly be interpreted.

CLAIMS EXCEEDING $90 MILLION

The collision took place approximately twenty miles west of *Nantucket* lightship on 25 July 1956 at approximately 2310. *Stockholm* had left New York at 1130 the same day heading for Gothenburg, having 534 passengers on board. In the collision, [fifty-one] persons died on *Andrea Doria* and five persons on *Stockholm*. The Italian vessel sank about 1000 the next day after more than 500 passengers and crew had been rescued by *Stockholm*. Over eleven hundred persons were rescued by other ships. *Stockholm* managed to return to New York where most of the people rescued were brought.

This casualty, of course, attracted a lot of media coverage, and there was much speculation as to the cause of the collision itself. Very soon it became clear that both shipping companies and their underwriters were faced with huge potential death, personal injury, property, and cargo claims. The aggregate of these claims was approximately $65 million. In addition, each shipowner had a claim against the other. The Italian company claimed $25 million for the lost vessel, and the Swedish company claimed $2 million for damage to *Stockholm*.

In order to avoid an arrest of the vessels and so as to provide security for all the above claims, it was necessary for each owner to deposit with the court in New York a sum of money in accordance with United States limitation law. This sum for *Andrea Doria* was in the region of $400,000 in respect of property damage and $1,550,000 regarding personal injury claims. As to *Stockholm*, the limitation amount was $3,900,000 regarding property damage and $640,000 for personal injury claims. At the same time, both shipowners filed petitions for exoneration from or limitation of liability. This really meant that both owners were suing each other. In view of the fact that this case was in federal court, all claims were dealt with in a comprehensive manner. It was for the court to decide issues of liability and whether the parties were entitled to limit their liability.

The case was settled by the shipowners and their underwriters in London in January 1957. Nevertheless, preparation for trial had been initiated when the limitation petitions were filed in New York. The District Court ordered that hearings commence in which the masters of the two vessels and their crews would testify. After this, they would be subjected to cross-examination. The court had appointed five special judges who shared the responsibility to oversee the proceedings. Scheduled to appear as witnesses were thirteen persons from *Stockholm* and sixteen persons from *Andrea Doria*.

The questioning of some witnesses took fifty-six days between 19 September and 14 December. In view of the London settlement, the preliminary hearing was never completed. These fifty-six days resulted in 5,650 pages of court transcripts. The fifty-six days only allowed for the questioning of both captains, one Swedish mate, and three Italian mates. The third mate of *Stockholm* had been subjected to cross-examination by the lawyers of the other side. He alone was in command that evening on the bridge, and he was subjected to a tough cross-examination which lasted about eleven days.

A "RADAR ASSISTED COLLISION"

From the outset the vessels seemed to be approaching each other almost head to head. The angle between the course lines did not exceed 4°, but it was enough so that each vessel saw the other's radar echoes on the opposite side. *Stockholm* saw the echo passing to port, and *Andrea Doria* saw the echo passing to starboard. These observations show the classic situation prior to a "radar assisted collision," and the two vessels followed the usual procedure. When they altered their headings, they did not turn away from each other but toward each other, resulting in a collision at high speed. This scenario is typical and has occurred in other less-well-known collisions.

According to testimony, *Andrea Doria* spotted the radar echo of *Stockholm* 4° to starboard at a distance of 17 miles. *Andrea Doria* had been in fog since 1500. The captain and two officers were on the bridge. One of the officers was serving as a radar lookout. The engine telegraph was on full speed, but due to the fog, the engine was on standby. This resulted in a reduction of pressure in the turbines from 40 kilograms to 37 kilograms which, in turn, resulted in a reduction in speed from 23 knots to 21.8 knots. The gyro compass indicated a course of 268° true. The automatic foghorn was being sounded.

The echo bearings and the distance information were reported constantly to the captain. No notes were taken and plotting was thought unnecessary. There was a plotting device on *Andrea Doria,* but it was stowed in a box on the bridge. In addition to the first observation of 17 miles starboard 4°, witnesses from *Andrea Doria* only recalled with certainty one observation, i.e., starboard 15°. Both watch officers claimed that the distance then was 3.5 miles and also stated that the captain was in error when he stated that it was 5 miles. It was thought on the basis of the observations that the vessels would pass each other starboard-to-starboard at a distance of 1 mile.

In sharp contrast to the testimony of the witnesses from *Andrea Doria,* the witnesses from *Stockholm* stated that *Stockholm* had good visibility, estimated at 5 to 6 miles. The captain had left the bridge, and the third mate was on watch. The echo of *Andrea Doria* was seen at about 12 miles distant. *Stockholm* was doing 18 knots—full speed. When the echo, after some minutes, was at 10 miles at 2° to port of the course line, a plot was laid out on the plotting board alongside the radar. The echo seemed to be approaching rapidly, and the bearing increasing slowly. A new plot was made with the plotting device, indicating a 6-mile distance, 4° bearing to port. The chief officer laid out the relative courses between the plotted positions. He found that the vessels should pass one another port-to-port at a distance of 0.7 to 0.8 miles and estimated that *Andrea Doria* was on an opposite course at a high speed.

Those on both ships had opposing opinions about the side on which the ships were going to pass, and this was maintained until the end.

On *Stockholm* the third officer remained at the radar. He had until now been unaware that the visibility had gotten worse, but he gradually realized that because he could not see the lights of another vessel, the ship was apparently proceeding at a very high speed in a fog. He therefore alerted the lookout, pressing him to try to see something to port. The distance between the ships was then decreasing, and when, according to the radar, it was down to 1.8 to 1.9 miles, suddenly a light turned up, bearing approximately 20° on the port bow. The lookout saw this simultaneously. The position of the light confirmed the mate's estimate that the vessels would pass each other port-to-port. He immediately ordered 20° to starboard. He then noted that *Andrea Doria* was turning to port, and therefore, gave the order of hard starboard and full astern on *Stockholm.* He heard the engine stop and then start to work in reverse just before the collision. At the same time, the engine telegraph rang and he heard a signal from *Andrea Doria.* This was the first and only signal heard by *Stockholm. Stockholm* did not sound any signals.

Just after the radar echo of *Stockholm* was seen at 3.5 miles, the captain of *Andrea Doria* ordered the course changed 4° port to 264°. The reason he did so was to try to increase the passing distance to more than 1 mile. When the echo of *Stockholm* was at a distance of 1.5 to 2 miles, still no foghorn signals were heard. Observations by radar had now been discontinued, and the captain and his two officers were trying to spot the lights on *Stockholm.* The glow from her lights showed up 20° to 40° to starboard at an estimated distance of approximately 1 mile. When the lights appeared more clearly, one could see that *Stockholm* was in a starboard turn and would proceed across the bow of *Andrea Doria.* In order to try to avoid a collision, *Andrea Doria* turned to port at

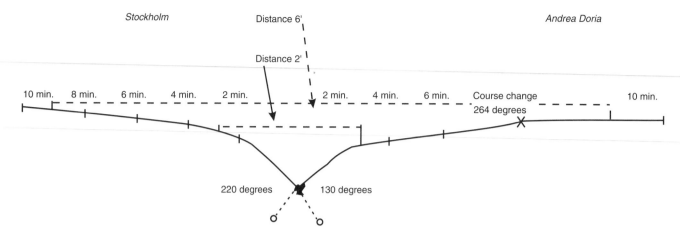

Stockholm   Distance 6'   *Andrea Doria*

Distance 2'

10 min.   8 min.   6 min.   4 min.   2 min.   2 min.   4 min.   6 min.   Course change   10 min.
264 degrees

220 degrees   130 degrees

Reconstruction according to the course recorder graphs. As shown in "A Radar Assisted Collision" by Captain Gustaf Ahrne, published by The Swedish Club, 1972.

full speed. The automatic foghorn signal was turned off, and a signal indicating a port rudder was then given.

Both vessels now headed southward toward one another. At 2309 according to the crew of *Stockholm,* or at 2310 according to the crew of *Andrea Doria,* the bow of *Stockholm* pierced and penetrated the starboard side of *Andrea Doria.* The collision angle was estimated between 65° and 100°. No one paid attention to the headings at the moment of impact. At the collision the speed of *Stockholm* had decreased, but *Andrea Doria* went at full speed past *Stockholm* with her damaged bow. Immediately after the collision, *Andrea Doria* began to list to starboard 18°. The listing gradually increased until she later, after eleven hours, sank.

The navigation documents from *Andrea Doria* were lost except for her course recorder graphs. On *Stockholm* the mate's plot disappeared. It had been erased the day after the collision when the plotting board was used for navigation on the way back to New York.

The course recorder graphs of both vessels were analyzed by Sperry, which was the manufacturer of these graphs, and by various maritime/technical experts in New York. They had estimated the turns made by both vessels up to the collision and had also es-

tablished that the course of *Stockholm* at the moment of collision was 132°. The heading at the moment of impact could not be seen on the graph of *Andrea Doria.* However, in view of the reported collision angle of 65° to 100°, and in view of the damage to the bow of *Stockholm,* one can assume the collision angle was in the region of 90°. The course of *Andrea Doria* at the time of collision should have been approximately 220 degrees. It is possible with the help of the turns to make a reconstruction, which by all means is not a perfect one, but which, at any rate, should give a truer view of the collision when compared with the testimony of the witnesses.

Approximately nine minutes before the collision, the distance between the vessels was 6 miles, and *Andrea Doria* then, according to the course recorder reconstruction, should have had the echo of *Stockholm* almost head on and not to its starboard which witnesses have claimed. (See illustration of course recorder graphs reconstruction.) Nevertheless, *Andrea Doria* turned 4° to port which resulted in the echo showing to starboard on the radar. The intention was to increase the passing distance, but the effect was exactly the opposite. A careful study of the situation, according to the course recorder graphs, revealed that the

    OUT OF THE FOG

changes of the bearings the whole time were considerably less than what the witnesses from *Andrea Doria* claimed. The accuracy of radar bearings at that time was ±2°. With a similar significant reading error, one could seem to observe a bearing increase of 4°, when, in reality, it was nonexistent. Excessive reliance on radar contributed to the catastrophe.

WHY DID *ANDREA DORIA* SINK?

The starboard list of 18°, which *Andrea Doria* developed immediately after the collision, increased gradually; after four hours, it was 35°. Just before she sank, the list had increased to 90°. The collision attracted such a degree of attention that the United States House of Representatives appointed a committee with the task of investigating whether *Andrea Doria* complied with the SOLAS Convention of 1948 and its requirement of watertight compartments and stability. The report of the committee was issued in December 1956. It was found that *Andrea Doria* just barely met the 1948 convention as to watertight compartments. She met the requirement of stability but only on condition that she was adequately ballasted. The convention required that a ship should maintain stability, even if she was damaged to a certain degree. It was established that *Andrea Doria*'s damage probably would have been less if she had met the stability requirements. The conclusion was made that *Andrea Doria* did not have enough ballast, thus resulting in instability. This was, on the balance of probability, the reason why she listed and eventually sank.

DID *STOCKHOLM* PROCEED IN THE WRONG TRACK?

During the testimony by the captain of *Stockholm,* it was claimed by the Italian owner that *Stockholm,* at the time of impact, was 19.5 miles north of where she should have been. She was steaming in the track recommended for vessels heading for New York. She should instead have followed another track for ships going east.

The 1948 SOLAS Convention recommended a separation of east- and westbound tracks. The United States Congress Committee also touched on this question and held that neither Sweden nor Italy was a party to the convention and was, therefore, not bound by it. However, in their report it was established that the collision would not have happened if *Stockholm* had chosen another track!

SETTLEMENT

The preliminary hearing showed that a trial in which liability and claims were tried would have been both protracted and expensive. Both vessels were, to a considerable degree, reinsured with various underwriters in London, and some of these entities had covered risks on both vessels. This meant that a long and protracted litigation would have entailed extra costs in view of the fact that the insurers would have had to pay compensation to both vessels, regardless of how fault was allocated.

From a public relations point of view, it seemed necessary to avoid a public trial since the preliminary hearing suggested that very harsh words would be uttered by both sides.

A first initiative was taken by the parties in mid-August in New York. This meeting was followed up by a quick meeting in Copenhagen among representatives of the two shipowners. It was agreed that the shipowners and their insurers should meet in London in January 1957 to discuss a settlement of all the claims.

This meeting was held on 9 and 10 January 1957. Present also were the London reinsurers of the two vessels. Two proposals were submitted. According to the Italian proposal, the only issue to be decided was whether to agree that both vessels should pay all acknowledged claims of passengers, crew, and cargo. The Swedish proposal, in contrast, was a settlement which included the damages of the two vessels. This proposal was accepted, and a written agreement was drafted accordingly.

This agreement meant that each vessel was to bear its own damages and that both parties would cooperate in reaching a swift resolution of all other claims. To accomplish this, it was necessary to establish a limitation fund in accordance with United States law. Sums remaining in the fund after all claims had been satisfied were to be handed over to the hull underwriters of *Andrea Doria*.

It was four years after the collision before all claims, in the region of $65 million, had been settled. Eventually, only $5.9 million was paid to claimants. Left in the fund was something more than $600,000 which was paid to the hull underwriters of *Andrea Doria*.

The settlement in London was solely a monetary settlement between the parties, but it also reflected the *de facto* apportionment of liability between the two vessels. The Italian owner had to bear 100 percent of the loss of *Andrea Doria,* and *Stockholm* had to bear its own repair costs. If one takes into account the whole settlement, one would end up with the following division of liability between the two vessels: 30 percent on *Stockholm* and 70 percent on *Andrea Doria*. There is no doubt that *Andrea Doria* was most at fault: her speed was too high, in view of her being in thick fog; her radar lookout was inadequate; and her maneuvers were wrong. *Stockholm,* on the other hand, should have realized that the visibility conditions were deteriorating. She should have decreased her speed and given fog signals before *Andrea Doria* was seen. She also should have given a signal before she turned to starboard.

Naval Architect's Report Regarding Stability of *Andrea Doria*

J. Lyell Wilson, SNAME

Report of subdivision and stability analysis of *Andrea Doria* on the basis of an inspection aboard her almost exact sister ship *Cristoforo Colombo*. The survey was requested by Charles Haight, attorney for the Swedish America Line. The inspection was done on October 7, 1956, by J. Lyell Wilson, a naval architect and member of the Society of Naval Architects and Marine Engineers.

GENERAL CHARACTERISTICS

Description: A twin-screw passenger liner built as a complete superstructure vessel, transversely framed, and having four continuous decks—upper or superstructure deck; foyer or freeboard deck; "A" or second deck; and "B" or lower deck. The strength deck or second (above freeboard deck) superstructure is the promenade deck which extends from the bow to the rudderpost or after perpendicular. The vessel is for the most part electrically arc-welded except for the longitudinal seams of the shell plating and is constructed of ordinary mild hull steel except for some topside reinforcements of special alloy strength steel. The top two (or four) tiers of deckhouse (above the promenade) have been built of a magnesium aluminum alloy for the purpose of reducing topside weight.

Subdivision: The hull is divided throughout its length into 11 watertight compartments by means of 10 watertight bulkheads extending up to the second or "A" deck, except that the collision bulkhead extends to the freeboard or foyer deck as required. The cellular double bottom extends all fore and aft between the fore and after peak bulkheads, and it is carried transversely around the bilge to merge with the wing tanks, in way of the machinery spaces, thus forming a double skin up to the "B" or lower deck from frame #105 at the after end of the engine room to frame #153 at the forward end of the generator room. With a factor of subdivision F-.35 (USA requirement) she is basically a 2-compartment vessel at the design draft of 30' 0".

Deep Tanks: Deep tanks are also provided at the forward and after ends of the main machinery spaces and just abaft the collision bulkhead. These forward extend transversely across the ship from shell to shell while the after group is divided on opposite wings of the shaft alleys with refrigerating machinery between the alleys.

Double Bottoms: The double-bottom tanks are divided transversely by watertight longitudinal girders in addition to the center vertical keep, except that the forward-most and aftermost of these are single centerline tanks with no longitudinal division, the center vertical keeps in way of these being nonwatertight. That in way of #2 hold (frames #173–196) and that in way of #3 hold (frames #40–60) are divided only by a watertight center vertical keep while all of the remaining double bottoms amidships are divided by watertight centerline and side girders so that there are four tanks abreast throughout this area. In addition there are sump tanks within the double bottom for lubricating oil and these are located at the forward end of the generator room and the after end of the engine room. In both groups they are separated by cofferdams on all four sides and from the bottom shell, the latter being at least 18 inches in depth, and all sumps are located at the centerline well inboard of the margin. Cofferdams are also fitted at frames #71–72, #104–105, #129–130 and at #173–174 separating oil from water tanks.

Longitudinal Divisions: Similarly, the deep tanks, which extend only to the platform or "D" deck level, are divided by longitudinal bulkheads corresponding generally with the double-bottom divisions and are similarly numbered with a different number for inboard and outboard tanks, port and starboard, of a specific group. Also, where there are four deep tanks abreast,

these are generally separated differently, between inboard and outboard groups, by transverse bulkheads at different frames, so that within a given compartment there are three (3) outboard deep tanks but only two (2) inboard deep tanks corresponding. The reason for such detailed explanation is apparent because of the fact that collision damage involved the group of 5 starboard deep tanks in way of the space between bulkheads #153 and #173. Cofferdams are also fitted to separate deep tanks intended for carrying oil from those intended for water and especially fresh and potable water which have complete surrounding cofferdams.

Wing Tanks: The wing tanks, which extend to the "B" deck, i.e., generally two decks higher than the deep tanks, are also fitted with cofferdams to isolate those intended for carrying reserve feed water in way of the boiler room.

Type of End Construction: Beyond the amidship wing tank area toward the ends, the double-bottom and side framing are of orthodox construction with a proper turned-down margin, tail bracket and side frame. Frame brackets and beam knees appear generally to be riveted.

Pipe and Access Tunnel in Deep Tanks: By far the most important feature of construction is the arrangement in way of the deep fuel oil tanks between bulkheads #153 and #173 in the compartment of subdivision with which the collision is primarily involved. The structural arrangements in this area violate the letter and intent of the International Convention for Safety of Life at Sea as interpreted by the United States Coast Guard Regulations for Passenger Vessels (CG-256 November 19, 1952).

Apparent Violation of Subdivision Requirements: The violation involves the omission of a power-operated sliding class 3 watertight door at the entrance to a pipe and access tunnel leading forward from the generator room commencing at frame #147, passing through bulkhead #153, just forward of which there are transverse laterals port and starboard extending to the wing bulkhead of the outboard tanks, and continuing on forward to another pair of transverse laterals and thence passing through bulkhead #173 into a valve control and pump room terminating at about frame #176. There are no doors of any kind in way of this tunnel, its laterals, and its terminating room, nor is there any escape trunk leading from it to a point above the "A" or bulkhead deck. It should be noted that the laterals (one on the forward side of bulkhead #153 and the other on the after side of bulkhead #173) are exactly like the centerline tunnel in size of cross section and are intended for access to the double-bottom tanks via their respective manholes in the tank top which forms the floor of the laterals. These laterals form a part of and are a continuation of the centerline part of the tunnel and it should be emphasized that the laterals, extending to the wing bulkheads of the outboard deep tanks #31 and #34 port and starboard and which form the ends of each such lateral, extend the tunnel toward each side shell so that it terminates, as a tunnel, apparently within 18 feet of the side shell whereas the convention requirement limits this distance to 1/5 the beam amidships which would be 18 feet. Therefore such a tunnel could not be exempt from the requirement for a watertight (class 3) door at frame #147 and an escape trunk to above "A" deck, even if it pierced but one of the subdivision bulkheads, i.e., either bulkhead #153 or bulkhead #173.

The foregoing data are based upon published information, which was relatively meager, and included very small-scale reproductions of several arrangement plans but without any transverse sections. A photostat copy of the midship section and of a forward end section were available after a preliminary set of lines had been developed from deck plans and faired with diagonals to give waterlines and equidistant transverse sections for estimating as much technical data as possible for analysis. These lines do not reflect the shape of the midship section and time did not permit revision but the differences are not too significant in causing appreciable error in preliminary calculations. While it is still impossible to reconcile certain differences among the small-scale photostatic plans available, the following results of technical analysis show a definite trend, though perhaps relative only, toward proving that the collision happened at just the right place to prove lack of proper stability and an apparent design error on *Andrea Doria*.

Displacement and Other Curves: These routine calculations were carried out mostly by Integrator but spot checks have shown them to be accurate within instrumentation error. The greatest concern involved longitudinal factors because of the apparently fuller body aft of amidships, especially the centers of flotation and, of course, the moment to change trim one inch. However, without these data the damaged stability calculations could not have been made in such a variety of conditions. Finished calculations made from actual plans should be made in the final analysis to ensure accurate results especially in such critical areas as the ends of the tunnel laterals for compliance with the convention requirements.

Bonjean Curves: Although a trim analysis did not seem warranted with an assumed set of lines as a basis, the half-section area curves were plotted anyway since the basic data were available from Integrator readings. The Bonjean curves therefore served mainly as a partial check on fairing of the body plan. The body plan itself was drawn in a form for developing cross-curves of stability but here again such a complete analysis did not seem justified even if sufficient time were available.

Damaged Stability: As interpreted by U.S. regulations, damaged stability was carried out principally to cover the flooding of the deep-tank compartment between bulkheads #153 and #173. When it became apparent that flooding more than one compartment would be claimed as the extent of damage, both compartments, generator room, and hold #2 were included, so that with all three flooded the extent of damage necessary became excessively high compared to any existing requirement.

Even though empirical relations were necessary, the results of the preliminary studies appear to justify their use. After all, they were the only alternative to the full analysis with accurate trim data, cross curves, and statical stability curves. To begin with, the condition of the ship on departure and for the voyage as to draft, loading, ballasting, etc., has not yet been made available. Therefore, it was possible only to analyze loss of stability and to try and fit the very few statements into the picture.

In any case, the approximations show clearly that lack of stability was a major cause of the sinking of *Andrea Doria*. If the metacentric height were as stated by Captain Calamai, then the initial angle of heel could not have been as great as he stated. He was probably on the low side with 18° immediate list to starboard and it probably was nearer 20°, which seems to be the average of most statements. However, 18° causes the margin line to come to the water only at about full-load draft, which would be difficult to understand or justify if the vessel were lacking in stability at just about her arrival condition.

Such matters cannot possibly be resolved without accurate and full analysis based upon accurate and full data and plans. The results obtained by preliminary estimate have, however, justified themselves in connection with discovery and in emphasizing the necessity for a proper analysis. Consideration should also be given to the problem as related to *Stockholm* which might be in question with regard to related characteristics.

APPENDIX D

Newsman Recalls *Andrea Doria* Tragedy for TV

Doug Fraser, Staff Writer

Reprinted from the *Cape Cod Times*, August 4, 2001.

THE HISTORY CHANNEL IS TAPING A DOCUMENTARY ABOUT THE SHIPWRECK THAT CLAIMED [56] LIVES.

ORLEANS—Black specks of dust, clinging to the 45-year-old newsreel footage, rain down like somber confetti as a ship emerges from a veil of fog.

Bill Quinn, a 33-year-old freelance video photographer from Orleans, was the first newsman to arrive at the ghastly shipwreck of the Italian luxury liner *Andrea Doria* and the Swedish liner *Stockholm*. After a short flight from Nantucket on July 26, 1956, Quinn documented the last great shipwreck of the golden age of transatlantic luxury liners at 7:45 in the morning.

This week, Quinn took a much longer flight—3,000 miles to Los Angeles to bear witness again, this time for a History Channel documentary featuring the wreck of the *Andrea Doria*. The program will air in January.

The collision occurred around 11:15 P.M. on July 25, 1956. Quinn received a heads-up from his brother Howard, a radio operator at the RCA station in Chatham. Howard Quinn had just transcribed a Morse code SOS from the stricken Italian liner.

The New York–bound Italian liner was homing in on a radio beacon from the *Nantucket* lightship. The beacon acted like airfield landing lights, keeping ships in the shipping lanes. Unfortunately, the Europe–bound *Stockholm* was also following the beacon, and the two ships closed on each other with a combined speed of 40 knots, colliding in the fog.

"WE'VE GOT TO GO"

"As a freelance cameraman, the guy who rings your phone first is the guy you're working for," Quinn said.

"You don't answer the phone, you don't have to work."

Quinn didn't wait for any phone call. He knew he had a big story and a jump on everyone else. He roused Wellfleet pilot Bill Ketchen from sleep with a curt "We've got to go."

At 12:15 A.M., they roared off from the grass airstrip of Orleans Skymeadow airfield in a twin-engine Cessna. Quinn expected to find the two liners lit up like Christmas trees in the inky water below. He had 100 feet of high-speed film loaded into a 16mm Bolex movie camera, which had to be manually wound.

Ketchen would have to make several passes for Quinn to shoot the roll.

Just past Nantucket, they hit the fog. A radio broadcast informed them the Coast Guard had closed the area. After an uneasy night on Nantucket, the two took off in the early morning, flying above the fog and clouds at 500 feet, dipping down to 50 feet off the water to take a look around. This time it was Quinn who made the call.

"We're depending on you," Ed Foy of WBZ TV news told the freelance cameraman.

They knew the wreck had happened 45 miles south of Nantucket, but even though a ship is the biggest thing man has ever put in motion, the ocean is a much bigger place. Other coordinates put the two ships 40 miles west of the lightship. Ketchen homed in on the lightship radio beacon then banked to the west skimming over the water at 50 feet until the ceiling lifted to 100 feet.

From 100 feet up in the air, the *Stockholm* emerged from the fog ghostly white,

its deck empty and portholes black. It was eerily becalmed on gentle summer seas. Two anchors, released by the force of the collision with the *Andrea Doria,* dangled from their anchor chains. The *Stockholm's* bow was blunted, like a snubbed cigar.

"The first thing I saw was the mangled bow. It looked like spaghetti. All you saw was a big jumbled mess," said Quinn.

Quinn went to work; as they flew past he tried shooting the ships from angles that best portrayed the tragedy. An armada of ships stood by, ready to give aid. Several lifeboats passed below.

ANDREA DORIA WAS A "SINKING JAIL"

"I didn't stop to think about how many people lost their lives. My job was to get the film. It was terribly cold and indifferent, but you think about the bad parts later," he said.

A second plane from the *New York Daily News* soon joined them.

After 20 minutes, Quinn had Ketchen swing the plane to the northwest and head for Logan Airport. Now it was a race to be the first to shore with the film.

With no sleep the night before, wearing the same shirt from two days before, and desperately needing a shave, Quinn was put on camera and interviewed by WBZ newsman Jack Chase as soon as he landed.

His eyes glued to the viewfinder of his Bolex movie camera, Quinn was unaware of the passengers trapped in their staterooms who were experiencing their final hours before they dropped 260 feet to the ocean bottom.

Quinn finally had time to think of the [51 people from *Andrea Doria*] lost in the collision when he covered a funeral for one of the victims. There were [over 1600] survivors. Forty-five years later, Quinn is still horrified by the thought.

"When I think about those poor people trapped aboard that vessel. It was just like being in a jail and having the jail sink," he said.

Following the footage of the *Stockholm*, the *Andrea Doria* appears through the fog, listing heavily to starboard, its massive propellers nearly clear of the water.

For the 2½ minute snippet of news film, Quinn received $100.

Sources

BOOKS

Hoffer, William. *Saved! The Story of Andrea Doria–the Greatest Sea Rescue in History.* New York: Summit Books, 1979.

Mattsson, Algot. *Westward Way (Vägen mot väster).* Stockholm: Askild and Kärnekulls Förlag, 1982.

Mattsson, Algot. *Floating Palaces: The White Viking Fleet.* Gothenburg: Tre Böcker Förlag, 1983.

Mattsson, Algot. *The Broström Concern: The Rise and Fall of a Dynasty.* Gothenburg: Tre Böcker Förlag, 1984.

Maxtone-Graham, John. *The Only Way to Cross.* New York: Collier Books, 1972.

Moscow, Alvin. *Collision Course.* New York: G.P. Putnam's Sons, 1959.

Quinn, William P. *Shipwrecks Around Cape Cod.* Farmington, Maine: Knowlton and McLeary Co., 1973.

NEWSPAPERS AND PERIODICALS

Swedish dailies (Metropolitan Press), July 1956 to March 1985:
    The Broström Concern's archives
    Maritime Museum, Gothenburg
    University Library, Gothenburg
    Author's private collection

American, English, and Italian newspapers:
    Author's private collection

Technical newspapers and periodicals:
    Maritime Museum, Gothenburg

MISCELLANEOUS

Minutes of preliminary hearing in New York:
    Maritime Museum archives
    Broström Concern's archives
    Author's private collection

Stability calculations regarding *Andrea Doria:*
    Broström Concern's archives
    Author's private collection

Correspondence
    Municipal archives in Gothenburg

Selected interviews

Index

The names Johan-Ernst Carstens Johannsen, Gunnar Nordenson, and Piero Calamai are mentioned throughout the book; their names are not included in this index.

Attorneys Charles S. Haight and Eugene Underwood are mentioned predominantly in the following chapters: